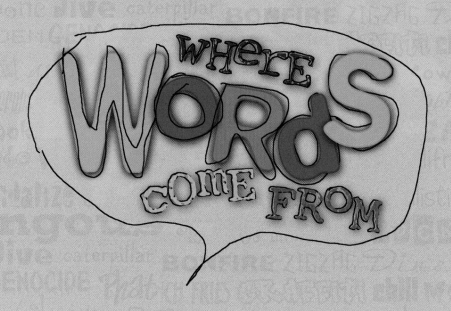

WHERE WORDS COME FROM

JACK UMSTATTER

Franklin Watts
A Division of Scholastic Inc.
New York • Toronto • London • Auckland • Sydney
Mexico City • New Delhi • Hong Kong
Danbury, Connecticut

For my wife, Chris, and my daughters,
Kate and Maureen, with love

and to my friend, Joe Tessitore,
with much appreciation

Photographs © 2002: AP/Wide World Photos/Mark Wilson: 129; Archive Photos/Getty Images: 139 (Ed Carlin), 132 bottom, 133 (Hulton Getty Collection), 72, 112; Corbis Images: 58, 59 (Paul Almasy), 91, 120 (Bettmann), 26 right (Gary W. Carter), 63 (Henry Diltz), 32 (Sandy Felsenhal), 21 left (Mitchell Gerber), 136 (Todd Gipstein), 127 (Helen Norman), 35 bottom (Fritz Polking/Frank Lane Picture Agency), 27 left (Vittoriano Rastelli), 135 bottom (Ted Steshinsky), 65 (Patrick W. Stoll), 81 (Ed Young), 47 bottom, 119 top; Envision: 96 (Grace Davies), 57 (Steven Mark Needham); Nance S. Trueworthy: 20, 43, 97, 142; NASA: 83; Peter Arnold Inc./Kelvin Aitken: 143; Photo Researchers, NY: 28 right (Scott Camazine), 10 (Jeff Greenberg), 46 (George Haling), 103 (Richard Hutchings), 135 top (Susan Leavines), 19 (Andy Levin), 64 top (Sven-Olof Lindblad), 55 (Tom McHugh), 15 (Joseph Nettis), 51 (Jerry Schad), 109 (B. Seitz), 126 (Sunstar), 84, 85 (Catherine Ursillo), 8 (Vision), 116, 117 bottom (Andrew G. Wood); Photodisc, Inc.: 45, 50, 95, 99, 108, 114; PhotoEdit: 31 top, 68, 131 (Robert Brenner), 48, 49 (Mary Kate Denny), 31 bottom (Amy C. Etra), 101, 149 (Myrleen Ferguson Cate), 21 right, 28 left (Tony Freeman), 106 (Robert Ginn), 111 (Spencer Grant), 27 right, 86 (Jeff Greenberg), 17 left (Felicia Martinez), 37, 89 (Tom McCarthy), 146, 147 (John Neubauer), 23, 47 top, 75 (Michael Newman), 40 (Dwayne Newton), 153 (Novastock), 117 top (Mark Richards), 124, 141 (Dana White), 54, 74, 123 (David Young-Wolff); Rigoberto Quinteros: 88, 118, 155; SODA: 76 (Richard Lee), 14 top, 22, 26 left, 39 right, 60, 61, 67, 70, 79, 104, 130, 132 top (Photodisc), 115 top (Salvatore Principato); Stone/Getty Images: 69 (Wayne R. Bilenduke), 92 (Vito Palmisano); Superstock, Inc./Palace of Versailles, France/Lauros-Giraudon, Paris: 94; Tom Bean: 138; United States Holocaust Memorial Museum/ State Archives of the Russian Federation: 52; Viesti Collection, Inc.: 93 right (Ingo Arndt), 151 (Walter Bibikow), 56 (Martha Cooper), 113 (S. Harris/TRIP), 80, 144 (Joe Viesti), 35 top (John W. Warden), 107 (Robert Winslow); Visuals Unlimited: 33 (R.F. Ashley), 14 bottom, 93 left (Jeff J. Daly), 29 (Kim Fennema), 17 right, 115 bottom, 119 bottom (Mark E. Gibson), 121, 152 (Jeff Greenberg), 64 bottom (Lynne Ledbetter), 38, 39 left (Ken Lucas), 150 (SIU), 36 (William J. Weber), 137 (Warren Williams), 53.

Book design by A. Natacha Pimentel C.

Library of Congress Cataloging-in-Publication Data
Umstatter, Jack.
      Where words come from / Jack Umstatter.
        p. cm. — (Watts reference)
      Includes bibliographical references and index.
      Summary: An alphabetical exploration of various words, both proper
and slang, explaining their origins, meaning, and changes in usage.
      ISBN 0-531-11902-5
1. English language—Etymology—Dictionaries, Juvenile. [1. English language—
Etymology—Dictionaries.] I. Title. II. Series.

PE1580 .U47 2002
422'.03—dc21
                                              2001024894

CONTENTS

INTRODUCTION

No one is exactly sure how language began, but we certainly can make some educated guesses as to how primitive people communicated. They probably used sounds to express basic emotions such as joy or fear. Gestures most likely accompanied these sounds. So when the cave man rubbed his stomach and made a sound such as "Ahh!," he was telling his companion that the meat from the animal he had recently captured was tasty. These ancients also used smoke signals, pictures, and codes to reveal their thoughts, emotions, needs, and other information. In this way, human beings began to define themselves and their surroundings, in much the same way that modern-day people do now.

Later, people moved from these very early means of communication to more advanced techniques. By associating something, say a dog, with its sound, say "woof," they began to formulate words. These imitative words are the distant relatives of today's *boom*, *swish*, and *whack*. Eventually, gestures, sounds, and newly created words were joined together as people exchanged stories and ideas. In this way, a "language" was formed as more and more words were created.

You are probably now asking, "Then where did the English language originate?" Ralph Waldo Emerson, the American essayist, poet, and philosopher, said, "The English language is the sea which receives tributaries from every region under heaven." English is really a combination of French, Latin, Greek, German, some Scandinavian languages, and several minor languages. It might initially sound silly, but you owe a debt of gratitude to these foreign speakers for your native tongue. These non-English speakers certainly influenced the development of the English language and, to a large extent, the words that you use every day.

English is undoubtedly the world's most important language. Walt Whitman, the renowned poet, stated, "The English language is the accretion and growth of every dialect, race, and range of time." There are approximately 1 million words in the English language. German has about 185,000, and French has nearly 100,000. More than 350 million of the world's 6 billion people use English as their primary language. Consider the fact that there are about 2,700 languages in the world, and you will see how prominent and influential the English language is!

Where Words Come From includes the definitions and colorful stories of nearly 400 of the most interesting words found in the English language. These words, presented in alphabetical order, come in all shapes, sizes, and flavors. There is a 2-letter word and there is a 34-letter word. Many of these words are borrowed from other languages (*boss, jeopardy,* and *Ouija® board*). Some are slang versions of other words (*dis, nuke,* and *wannabe*). You will also be introduced to words named for people (*Graham cracker, sandwich,* and *teddy bear*) and words named for geographical locations (*hamburger, napoleon,* and *rugby*). Even some common

(*AWOL* and *IOU*) and not so common (*NIMBY*) abbreviations are here. Most of the book's entries include a concluding sentence or two that will help you remember both the word's definition and its history. These interesting and enjoyable stories will help you to increase your vocabulary as you gain a greater interest in learning the stories behind these words and other words you encounter in the future.

Where Words Come From provides the answers to some intriguing questions about words. Does *Adidas* really mean "*All day I dream about soccer?*" Where did the *months* of the year get their names? Is a *bikini* really named after a group of islands? Why do we call the weight-lifting device a *dumbbell?* Can you eat *humble pie?* Where did baseball's famed *seventh-inning stretch* begin? Why do the *bleacher* seats in baseball parks have that name? How responsible were bakery workers for the *Frisbee®*'s popularity? What does a *curfew* have to do with an indoor fire? Does the lion have anything to do with the *dandelion?* Why are some motorists and passengers called *rubbernecks?* What common trait do *airheads* and *blockheads* share? Who gave us the word *Scrooge?* How old is the word *robot?*

The entries in *Where Words Come From* span many centuries and provide a picture of the English language's evolution. They also help to define who we are because the words we use and the way we use them tell much about us. In a sense, you will learn more about other people, past and present. Perhaps you will even learn more about yourself! So sit back and enjoy the fascinating stories behind the words found in *Where Words Come From*. You just might be in for a few surprises!

Adidas Many people believe that the name for this athletic equipment company is derived from the first letters of the six words in the sentence, "*All day I dream about soccer.*" Actually, the name of this company known for its running shoes comes from the first three letters in both names of the company's founder, *Adi Dassler*. Another popular running shoe company, Nike, is named in honor of the Greek winged goddess of victory. Interestingly enough, the name of another well-known company, Xerox, is from the Greek word for dry since the reproduced copies made by a Xerox machine are exactly that—dry.

aerobics Started in the late 1960s, *aerobics* was a conditioning program invented to keep America's astronauts fit by closely monitoring their pulse rates and oxygen use. At that time, Americans, using more automated machinery than ever before, needed more exercise. A less formal style of the programmed exercise routine called *aerobics* became popular and gave people, especially the *couch potatoes* and *junk food* lovers, a road to greater fitness. Today, with air-conditioned health clubs, fit *aerobics* instructors, and invigorating music, *aerobic* activities are a fun way to become fit.

An aerobics class

aftermath You may hear a news reporter (*talking head*) say, "The flood's *aftermath* (that which results from or follows an event) will be quite costly." Five hundred years ago, *aftermath* was spelled after*mowth* (the second or later mowing). This *after mowth* was the crop of grass that grew after the first mowing in the early summer. Most of the time today, an *aftermath* follows an unpleasant event such as a natural disaster. What is the *aftermath* of pigging out on *junk foods* just before you go to bed at night?

airhead (*slang*) One who is not very intelligent may be called an *airhead*. Whether the term came from the fact that this rather intellectually dull person's head was "out there in space" or "filled with air," this slang expression became quite popular in the later decades of the 1900s. Interestingly enough, an *airhead* and a *blockhead*, though seemingly antonyms because one is empty and one is filled, essentially mean the same thing. Even an *airhead* might understand that!

alphabet The word *alphabet*, the sequential letters of any language, is made by combining the first (*alpha*) and the second (*beta*) letters of the Greek *alphabet*. It is that simple!

Although you already know the twenty-six letters of the English alphabet, you can now memorize all twenty-four letters of the Greek *alphabet*! Let's start. *Alpha, beta...*

Amazon *Amazons* were mythical female warriors. The Greeks combined the prefix "-a" (without) and the root "*mazos*" (breast) to form what we now know as *Amazon*. This seems appropriate because these fearsome women supposedly cut off their breasts so that they could pull back the bow and shoot their arrows more effectively in battle. Some word historians say that the name could also be a combination of "*a*" (not) and "*maza*" (cereal food), which would also be fitting since these toughies primarily ate meat. Now chew on those two stories for a while!

April Long ago, *April* was the second month of the calendar. It was named in honor of Venus, the Roman goddess of love and beauty. The word *April* is a form of the earlier *Aprilis*, which came from *aperia*, the Latin word for "open." During the month of April, the spring buds open and become beautiful— much like the beauty of Venus.

A basketball arena

arena The modern *arena* hosts various sporting, musical, and circus events. How times have changed! Thousands of years ago, spectators witnessed bloody battles between gladiators in public shows held in Roman amphitheaters. There slaves fought each other or animals. Because the blood flowed quite freely in these encounters (as spectators cheered along), the ground of the amphitheater had to be covered with absorbent "*arena*," the Latin word for sand. In time, *arena* replaced amphitheater as the name of this bloody battleground. Thankfully, today's *arenas* feature calmer events.

assassin Nearly 1,000 years ago, there lived a murderous group of religious fanatics who killed their political foes. For two centuries, this Muslim group, supposedly under the influence of hashish (an intoxicating drug), secretly slaughtered the Christian crusaders traveling to the Holy Land. These Near Eastern *hashshashins* (hashish-eaters) allegedly used the drug to ready themselves to kill the crusaders. Today, *assassins*, the modern-day *hashshashins*, are killers of politically important persons. An *assassin* killed President John Fitzgerald Kennedy in Dallas on November 22, 1963.

assassin

"Procrastination is opportunity's natural **assassin**."
—Victor Kiam (U.S. businessman)

athlete

athlete In ancient Greece an "*athlon*" was the prize given to those who competed in physical activities that were part of the public games. From "*athlon*" came the English word *athlete*. For many modern-day *athletes*, the "*athlon*" might be a gold medal—or a rich, long-term contract.

athlete

"Desire is the most important factor in the success of any **athlete**."
—Willie Shoemaker (U.S. jockey)

Atlas In Greek mythology, *Atlas* was a powerful Greek god who was forced to support the heavens on his shoulders. During the 1500s, Gerardus Mercator, a map maker, used the picture of a strong man, almost a godlike person, holding the globe on his back as the front drawing for his collection of maps. People mistakenly thought this strong man to be *Atlas*, and so the word *atlas* as a book or collection of maps was born.

attitude *Attitude* used to simply mean one's manner of feeling, one's opinion, or one's mental set. A person could have a positive *attitude* toward life. Since the 1980s, *attitude* has also been associated with a sense of arrogance. Thus, "He's got *attitude* (or '*tude*)," could mean "He's cocky (or overly proud, self-important, rude)." People never want *attitude* from others!

attitude

"I guess I was never much in awe of anybody. I think you have to have that **attitude** if you're going to go far in this game."
—Bob Gibson (Hall of Fame pitcher)

August   This month was originally named *Sextilis*, meaning sixth. Caius Julius Caesar Octavianus, nephew of the slain Julius Caesar, was a skilled war general, brilliant governmental official, and popular figure among the ancient Roman people. In 27 B.C. (Before Christ), after two years as the ruler of the entire Roman Empire, this Caesar was given the title *Augustus*, meaning "awesome and magnificent." In 8 B.C., the Roman senate members renamed these thirty-one days *August* to honor their great leader, *Augustus* Caesar. Both *July* (Julius Caesar) and *August* are named after famous Roman Empire leaders.

awesome   California's surfers used "awesome" to describe any "really cool" thing, such as an "*awesome* wave." Originating in California's San Fernando Valley in the late 1970s and early 1980s, "*Valley Girls*" were those, often wealthy, teenagers who hung out at the mall and spoke their rather unique language filled with words such as "fer sure" and "gross me out!" Actually, these girls borrowed many of their words and expressions from these surfers. *Awesome* was one such word. For these "*Valley Girls*," *awesome*, which really means "inspiring a feeling of wonder," was used to describe *almost* anything (or everything) that was cool. After all, do so many everyday things and events truly inspire awe? Obviously, *awesome* was overused then and, some may argue, is still overused today. Now, isn't that an *awesome* idea, *dude*!

AWOL   Civil War soldiers who left their assigned guard posts or battlefield positions without permission were "*a*bsent *w*ithout *l*eave." These men were usually gone for only a short period of time. Yet, if a soldier deserted the Confederate Army (the South), he was forced to wear a sign bearing the large letters *AWOL*, a brand of disgrace. Starting with World War II (1939-1945), *AWOL* was pronounced as if it were a word (AY-wall). When students "skip out of school" or "cut," they are certainly *AWOL*.

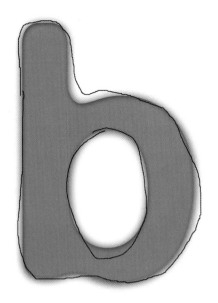

babble According to the ancient scripture, at one time there was only one language in the whole world. That changed when the people of the city called *Babel* tried (unsuccessfully) to build a tower to reach God in heaven. They were punished when God, unhappy with their intentions and actions, created many tongues (languages) so that these citizens were unable to communicate with each other. Today, *babble* (a form of *Babel*), is confusing, silly speech. Speak clearly, and do not *babble*!

babble

"The answer is not to stop worrying about what you eat, but to sort out the sound advice from the **babble**."
—Linda Kulman in her article "Food News Can Get You Dizzy, So Know What to Swallow," U.S. News & World Report, *November 13, 2000, pp. 68-72*

babe (*slang*) In the 1930s, a *babe* was an attractive girl. Several decades later, a *babe* could also mean an attractive guy. More recently, *babe*, thanks to the characters Garth Algar and Wayne Campbell of the movie, *Wayne's World*, and the television program, *Saturday Night Live*, has enjoyed unprecedented popularity. After all, those *dudes* Garth and Wayne gave us words such as *Babe*-elonia, *babe*-a-tude, and *babe*-osity. What would baseball legend Babe Ruth say about Garth and Wayne's *babes*?

baby boom Between the end of World War II (1945) and the early 1960s, there was a huge increase in the number of babies born in the United States. These infants became part of the single largest group of babies born in America. They made up the *baby boom* (great increase) generation. During this period of almost 20 years, many Americans enjoyed a period of financial prosperity and well-being, for, by and large, they were the "happy days" of the 1950s. Subsequently, when these *baby boomers* became adults, many enjoyed even greater wealth than their parents had known. After all, their parents were children during the Great Depression (1929 through most of the 1930s).

These *baby boomers* were the first generation of children to watch television and dance to a new type of music called *rock and roll*. As young adults, some attended Woodstock, the renowned 1969 music festival. Who are the *baby boomers* in your family?

bad (*slang*) To the Beat Generation of the 1950s, a *bad* event was a cool (or good) time. This *fantabulous*, *fat*, or *oogley* (all Beat Generation words) event was really dynamite or cool, man! Within ten years, *bad* also came to mean something truly bad. So if something was *bad*, it could be *boss*, *groovy*, *swingin'*, or *tuff* (meaning good), or it could be ugly (meaning bad). Today's hip-hoppers and rappers use *bad* to mean something good. Confusing enough? That's too *bad*. Or is it too good?

badminton This racket game, invented by people in India and played by the British, is named for *Badminton*, the Duke of Beaufort's estate. The British have been playing *badminton* for over 200 years. How well did the Duke watch (and hit) the *badminton* birdie on his estate? Who knows? No matter what, he really had a racket at *badminton*.

Bagel

bagel What do a *bagel* and a bracelet have in common? Easy! Both come from the German word *bouc* (bracelet-like in shape). Don't confuse the two. Eat the *bagel*. Wear the bracelet.

Badminton set

14

ballot Some ancient governments, notably those of Greece and Rome, did not allow every citizen to vote. Slaves, women, those who did not own property, and those who were citizens, though not native born, did not enjoy voting privileges. Since some of the Roman voters were illiterate, instead of writing out their votes, they voted using a white ball (for yes) or a black ball (for no). This little voting ball (*ballotta* in Latin) is now the English word *ballot*—the ticket, paper, electronic device, or other means by which a vote is registered. Instead of the *ballotta* used by the Romans, the Greeks used either shells, pebbles, or beans to cast a vote. The Greek vote counters might be the original *bean counters*, a modern, rather insulting term meaning those whose job requires them to submit detailed reports on the money spent and earned by a company. *Ballots* were at the center of the controversy as to whether George W. Bush or Al Gore won the United States Presidential election in 2000.

ballot

"The **ballot** is stronger than bullets."
—*Joseph Schumpter in* Capitalism, Socialism, and Democracy

bangs Both boys and girls sport *bangs*, the short, straight, and squared-off front hair that rests on the forehead. Since the stable boys who were in charge of grooming horses were often pressed for time, they would often "whack the hair off" or "bang off" the end of the horse's tail. In time, this banging gave the name "bangtails" to this hair arrangement. These "bangs" were often the style of many champion racehorses of the day and may have contributed to the hairstyle's popularity. Ponytails, pigtails, poodle cuts, crew-cuts, feather cuts, ducktails, and Afros are other hair styles that have been popular at one time.

A girl with bangs

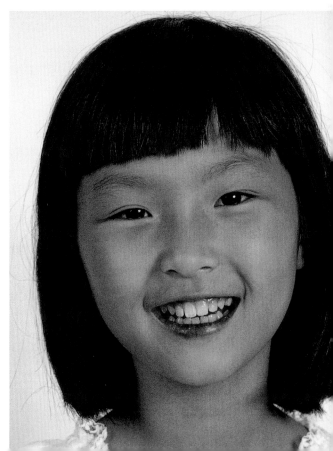

bank Medieval Italian money-lenders conducted their business dealings on small, narrow benches in the marketplace. These benches or *bancas* later became the English word *banks*. If the Italian moneylenders failed in their business, they were forced to break up their *bancas*. This action, called *banca rupta*, is the modern-day *bankrupt*.

Since today's bankers use desks and counters in their daily business transactions, it would be hard to find a bench in any *bank* today. You can *bank* on that!

bedlam Today, *bedlam* means a disorderly scene as in "The soccer stadium turned into a scene of *bedlam* when the opposing fans started throwing rocks and bottles at each other." The word *bedlam* began with St. Mary of *Bethlehem*, a London insane asylum, about 800 years ago. (St. Mary's later became a hospital for the mentally ill.) The asylum's wards were full of noise and confusion. When Londoners, largely because of their dialect, pronounced *Bethlehem*, the word sounded much like the way we pronounce *bedlam* today. In this way, *Bethlehem* became forever linked with *bedlam*—and noisy, confusing scenes.

belly A human being's *belly* or abdomen, the lower front part of the body located between the chest and the waist, has its word origin in an old word *belig* meaning skin bag. A *belig* (though not part of the human body) was used to store or carry foods such as peas and beans. Later, *belig* took on the idea of "to swell" or "to inflate," as what a belly might appear to do. *Bellybutton* (colloquial for the navel), *bellyache* (to complain), *belly laugh* (a hearty laugh), and *belly flop* (an awkward type of dive) are other words associated with *belly*. Ships, animals, and even some musical instruments even have *bellies*.

bikini This popular, attractive two-piece women's bathing suit was a big hit in the 1940s. At the same time, the *Bikini* atoll (a ring-shaped coral island) in the North Pacific Ocean was the scene of the atomic bomb's testing. Fashion experts noted that men, seeing this skimpy bathing suit for the first time, were quite taken by the outfit. The noise generated by the atomic bomb and the sight of a woman in a *bikini* had the same effect on the men. Both were explosive!

birdie In the mid-1800s, bird was a slang for someone or something of excellence. A girl's boyfriend could have been described as a "perfect bird of a lad." Since bird came to be associated with excellence, it was only a matter of time before bird also became part of golf's vocabulary.

In golf, a "*birdie*" is "one stroke under par" (a skillful score). Even better is the *eagle*, two strokes under par! Though a *birdie* is pretty good, an eagle soars even higher than a *birdie*.

biscuit

Next time you bite into a delicious *biscuit*, think twice. Twice? Yes, because years ago seamen cooked *biscuits* twice to prevent them from spoiling during the long sea voyages. *Biscuit*, a word given to us by the French, means "cooked twice." What would those seamen do if they had microwaves? Think twice about that!

Biscuits

blackball

To *blackball* someone is to cast a vote against a person's admission into a group or society or to exclude that person. The ancient Romans voted with *ballottas* or voting balls. The white ball signified a yes vote, and the black ball registered a no vote of a candidate or a proposal.

Receiving more black ball votes than white ball votes (*blackballing*) signified the voters' disapproval. Today, a *blackball* is a harsh form of disapproval.

bleachers

What do linens on a clothesline and the wooden benches in the uncovered, outdoor sections of a baseball park have in common? Both are exposed to the sun—and both, in a sense, become *bleached*. So, in the late 1800s, the name *bleachers* was given to those ballpark benches on which the sun shines most. Still today, those fans sitting in the *bleachers* have a chance to work on their tans and see a game at the same time! What a ball!

Bleachers

blind date During America's Roaring Twenties, *blind date* was the term used to describe either the person (one whom you had not formally met) who would accompany you on a social occasion or the event or date itself. With a *blind date*, another person "set up" the date between the two strangers who were unknown or "blind" to each other until they met on that date. Though the *blind date* is not as common today as it was during the 1920s, it is still part of the social scene. Would you ever go on a *blind date*? Hmmm … let's see.

blockhead In the 1300s, hat makers used head-shaped blocks of wood for designing and fitting the hats they made. These heads of wood or *blockheads* helped the hat makers find the exact fit. During the reign of Henry VIII (1491-1547), unintelligent people were referred to as *blockheads* since, according to some, their heads contained no more brains than the hat makers' blocks of wood. Maybe that is why people today say that unintelligent people have sawdust for brains.

bloomers In the mid-1800s, Amelia Jenks *Bloomer*, a vocal women's rights spokesperson and a supporter of the well-known reformer, Susan B. Anthony, fought passionately for a woman's outfit made up of a short skirt over loose trousers gathered at the ankles. Though not the outfit's inventor, *Bloomer* claimed that this shortened apparel was liberating and more sanitary (the longer skirts picked up dirt and other debris from the unpaved streets). "What is good for the male is good for the female" was *Bloomer*'s philosophy. This new attire was initially called the "*Bloomer* costume" and then popularly known as *bloomers* when women wore this outfit during the bicycle-riding craze of the 1890s.

bloomers

"She (100-year-old Hatsy) remembers riding in her father's horse-drawn wagon and singing around the piano and swimming in long, concealing **bloomers**."

—Katy Read in her article, "The Centenarians," in Times-Picayune (New Orleans, LA), March 14, 1993, pp. D1+

blue laws Ever wonder why certain items cannot be purchased on Sundays or why certain stores are closed on Sundays? The answer just might be "*blue laws*." During the late 1600s, moralistic, colonial New Englanders passed laws (*blue laws*) restricting or banning certain behaviors. These moral laws were then widened to include specific business activities on Sunday, which was designated the

Lord's Day. Allegedly, the paper that these laws were written on was *blue*. Even today in certain parts of America, some forms of activities and the sale of alcoholic beverages are prohibited on Sundays. Would people be *blue* if additional *blue laws* were instituted?

blues Those who sang a type of music called the *blue devils* almost 300 years ago paved the way for today's *blues* singers. *Blue devils* expressed the same depression, hopelessness, and despair that the African American religious songs called spirituals did. Coined in 1911, the more modern *blues*, a shortened form of *blue devils*, served the same purpose as its ancestor. Interestingly enough, *blues* features many blue notes (slightly flattened notes). If you "sing the *blues*" when things are not going well for you, does the *blue devil* make you do it?

bogus (*slang*) Quite simply, today the word *bogus* means not genuine. You could hear about a "*bogus* (not genuine) bracelet" or a "*bogus* (insufficient or not good) answer." The original *bogus* was a coin. Two hundred years ago, the word *boko* (a fake coin) was part of the Hausa language of West Africa. At that time, those Africans brought to America as slaves probably brought this word (that later became *bogus*) with them. And that's no *bogus* story!

bonfire Today a *bonfire* is a large fire, usually built outdoors and associated with happy occasions, such as a football rally or a town's celebration.

Bonfire

Interestingly enough, a *bonfire* was not always tied to happiness. About 600 years ago, what we know today as a *bonfire* was called a *banefire*, but it was really a *bone*fire since dead bodies were burned in these outdoor fires. During English King Henry VIII's reign (1509-1547), saints' corpses were burned in these fires, and believers would hunt for the saints' sacred bones in the smoldering remains of the fire. Aren't you glad that times have changed?

boom box

(*slang*) The portable tape player with powerful speakers known as the *boom box* (or box or boom) became popular in the 1970s in many large urban American cities. Its popularity has certainly spread since then. The music, often *rap music*, would be *boomed* or blasted through these strong speakers. *Break dancers* and *rappers* would use the *boom box* as musical accompaniment during their performances. Today, members of the older generation whose ears are not as tolerant of the loud music usually do not share the younger generation's attraction to the *boom box*. To them, it is not a booming success!

Boom box

bootleg

More than 100 years ago, for different reasons, people smuggled (brought, took, or carried secretly and illegally) objects, especially liquor, that they had hidden in the *leg* of their high *boot*. Today, *bootleg* means to make, carry, or sell secretly and illegally. A *bootleg* is also something that is made in the same illegal way, such as making a *bootlegged* CD—one made without the music publisher's permission. Lastly, when a football quarterback fakes a handoff to a running back and then runs around the end hiding the ball behind his hip, he is performing a *bootleg*. Now, as you can see, there is nothing hidden in *bootleg*'s history.

boss

The Dutch word *baas* means "master." In the 1600s and 1700s, many Dutch lived in New York. The city was even called New Amsterdam after the Dutch capital. In those days people who knew a trade were called masters, and those learning a trade were called apprentices. After the Dutch word *baas* was adopted by English speakers, its spelling changed to *b-o-s-s*. The word's meaning also changed so that it now refers to anyone who supervises the work of other people. The beatniks and hippies used the slang *boss* to describe anyone or anything really cool. It would be really *boss* if you could master *boss*'s history.

box To *box* means to strike with the hand or fist, especially on the ear or side of the head, is to *box*. Thus, the sport that features competitors striking each other is appropriately named boxing. A boxer, the square, short-haired dog known for its fighting abilities, uses its front paws in a fight much like a boxer uses the hand or fist in a boxing match. Muhammad Ali, Joe Louis, and Rocky Marciano are three of boxing's all-time greats. These men were striking athletes!

Boxer Muhammad Ali

Braille This system of writing and printing for the blind uses raised dots felt by the fingers. More than 200 years ago, a French Army captain invented a system of raised dots and dashes used by soldiers to send out and receive secret messages. In the 1830s, nine-year-old Louis *Braille* was blinded in his father's shop while using an awl, a small, pointed tool used for making holes in wood and leather. Several years later, *Braille* improved the French captain's system by formulating a system called *Braille*. The blind still use that system today. Helen Keller was a famous blind person who used *Braille*.

This book is written in Braille

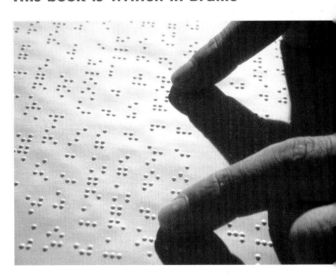

brain-dead (*slang*) This term is used to describe the condition of a person who is extremely tired. *Brain-dead* came from the idea that the individual was so fatigued that his brain was no longer functioning. Curiously enough, there is no term *brain-alive* to mean wide-awake. Have you ever been that tired that you could be called *brain-dead*?

brainwash

The Chinese combination of "hsi" (brain) and "nao" (wash) gave us our word for *brainwash*. Americans began to use this word in the early 1950s since it accurately described the techniques, including torture, threats, and intense questioning, used by the Chinese Communists against the American POWs (prisoners of war) in the Korean War. These captors tried to *brainwash* POWs (i.e., radically change the soldiers' thinking so they would be disloyal to the American cause). In this way they also hoped that the captured soldiers would divulge information about the American war forces and tactics. Today, some cults (rabid followers of a system of beliefs) employ forms of *brainwashing*.

brand-new

Originally, a *brand* was a flame or fire. When a product was *brand-new*, it was, supposedly, fresh out of the *brand* (fire). A blacksmith forged horseshoes in this hot *brand*. These would appropriately be called *brand-new* horseshoes. Often people mistakenly associate the word *brand* in *brand-new* with the *brand* name of the product, such as *Adidas* or *Nike*. Unfortunately, though this idea is neither hot nor *brand-new*, it is incorrect!

bread

(*slang*) Since the mid-1800s *bread* has been a slang word for money. Why? We all know that *bread*, a basic food, is made from dough. Money, like *bread*, is another of life's necessities because without it one would find it very hard to exist. So since we need both money and *bread*, these two words were used interchangeably. A flapper or dancer of the Roaring Twenties might purchase a loaf of *bread* with her *bread*. Confusing? *Bread*'s popularity and usage continued on into the beatnik, hippie, and rap eras. During the Great Depression, *bread* was not as plentiful as it was during the technology-driven profitable days of the 1990s.

Bread

break dancing

An old jazz term, *break* signified the time when the singer stepped away from the microphone and allowed the music and dancing to continue. In the latter part of the 1900s, the hip-hop culture gave the word *break* additional life. *Break dancing*, a fad of the late 1970s and 1980s, originated in the Bronx, a borough of New York City. Such dancing required athletic skills, acrobatic abilities, and terrific stamina. Appreciative sidewalk crowds that watched these dancers would sometimes tip the dancer or *breaker*. A form of street art similar to the work of magicians, mimes, and jugglers, *break dancing* also contributed other words to the English language. A *crew* was a group of *breakers*. The *breaker*'s sneakers were *dogs*; the performance attire was the *gear*. And now we will take a break from the *break dancing*.

buck (*slang*) Over 250 years ago, the Indians and the European settlers in America used a *buck* (deerskin) as a unit of value in trading. A strong horse or powerful mule was worth a certain number of *bucks*. So was a hat or a piece of clothing. During the 1900s, since deerskins were no

Breakdancer

longer used as often in exchanges, the *buck* gave way to the dollar as the exchange unit. Yet a dollar was still called a *buck*. And there's a *buck*'s worth of the *buck*'s history.

buck

"It's easy to make a **buck**. It's a lot tougher to make a difference."

—Tom Brokaw (U.S. broadcast journalist)

buckle The Latin *buccula*, a form of *bucca* (cheek), was the original name for the cheek strap holder on the battle helmets worn by Roman soldiers. Later, the word was extended to include *buckle* as a belt fastener. A soldier "*buckled* himself" when he fastened his armor cheek strap before going to battle. Nowadays, "to *buckle* down" means to set to work with a determined effort. Do you *buckle* down to do well in school?

buddy The history of this colloquial (informal) name for a close friend has several interesting stories. For the past 150 years, the word *buddy* has been used to designate a friend or companion. Why? Since youngsters often have difficulty pronouncing certain letters, the word brother might easily (and frequently) be pronounced *budda* or *buddy*. Another explanation of how *buddy* became an English word tells of how British coal miners in the late 1700s used *buddy* (perhaps spelled *butty* or *buddie*) to address a fellow worker. Still another account is that a booty fellow was an accomplice who shared in the booty or stolen goods. Over time, booty became *buddy*. A bosom *buddy* is a dear friend. Two or more people working together are often paired in a *buddy* system. "*Buddy*, can you spare a dime?" was a question often heard during the Great Depression (late 1929 through the 1930s), a time when a *buddy* in need was a *buddy* indeed.

bunk (*slang*) The word *bunk* originally meant a long-winded talk about nothing. Congressman Felix Walker from Buncombe County, North Carolina, once delivered a long and pointless speech before his congressional colleagues. Was Walker trying to fool them with his Buncombe type of speech? Surely, the other congressmen thought the speech was pure nonsense. Before long, *bunk*, the shortened form of Buncombe, came to mean something that was pointless, useless, and bad. And that explanation is no *bunk*!

bush league In the early 1900s, *bush league* was baseball's minor league. This league's players were inferior to the major league players. Originally, the Dutch gave us our word for *bush* meaning *wilderness*. In 1909, minor league baseball teams were located in the wilderness or bush—far from the cities where major league baseball was played. Today, *bush league* (or bush) means any small or second-rate activity. So let's be classy and stay away from *bush league* behaviors.

candidate We should be thankful that today's political *candidates* (those seeking public office) do not follow all the campaign strategies of their Roman political ancestors. In ancient Rome, those campaigning for public office wore a white toga (robelike garment) that had been rubbed with white chalk to make it whiter. Why this outfit and why the chalk? Supposedly, the toga meant that the *candidate* had a spotless reputation and was, therefore, worthy of election. *Candidate*, signifying the person running for political office, was first used in the 1600s. Today, the word has taken on meanings beyond politics. There are also job *candidates* and *candidates* for prestigious awards such as the Nobel Prize and the Pulitzer Prize. How much does a spotless reputation influence today's political *candidate*'s chances of winning an election?

canopy *Konops* is the Greek word for gnat. Long ago, along the Nile River in Africa, when fishermen needed to protect themselves from those annoying gnats and other insects, they erected a "gnat curtain" (*konops*) using meshed nets. Little did these fishermen realize that they had erected the first *canopy*—a sheltering structure or rooflike covering.

canter Canterbury is a city in England. It is also the site of the shrine of St. Thomas Becket, the Archbishop of Canterbury who was murdered by King Henry II's men in the late 1100s. Since the murder took place inside Canterbury Cathedral, many people considered the site a shrine and a holy place and made pilgrimages to Canterbury to honor Becket's memory. Many of the pilgrims made the trip on foot, and others atop horses would travel at a leisurely pace. This "Canterbury gallop" or "Canterbury trot" gave birth to the word *canter*, meaning "to ride at a smooth, easy pace like a moderate gallop." Can you remember *canter*'s history smoothly and easily?

cappuccino This Italian espresso coffee with steamed milk is probably named after the habit (part of a religious costume) worn by the French Capuchin monks more than 700 years ago. Care for a *cappuccino* to go, Brother Capuchin?

A cup of cappuccino

cardigan A *cardigan* is a sweater or jacket made of knitted wool. It opens down the front, is usually long-sleeved, and has no collar. James Thomas Brudenell, the seventh Earl of *Cardigan*, often wore this garment, and so it was appropriately named the *cardigan*. Brudenell, also an English general, led the famous charge of the Light Brigade in the Crimean War (1853-1856). Another piece of clothing named after a famous person is the Nehru jacket named after Jawaharlal Nehru, India's prime minister from 1947-1964. Will they ever name an article of clothing after you?

cardinal A *cardinal* has long been an important official in the Roman Catholic Church. A group of *cardinals* elects the pope, the highest-ranking church official. The name *cardinal* is from the Latin word, *cardo* (hinge). The pope's election depends (or hinges) on the votes of these *cardinals*. In addition, the bright-red crested bird called the *cardinal* is named after the religious *cardinal*'s bright red hat. Remember this story when you watch the St. Louis *Cardinals* baseball team and see their uniforms with the bright red letters.

A Roman Catholic Cardinal (right) and a cardinal bird (below)

It preceded the forty days of fasting and abstaining called Lent (Ash Wednesday to Easter Sunday). The *carnival* ended with Fat Tuesday or Mardi Gras, followed by almost seven weeks of strict dieting. So Mardi Gras was the last hurrah!

Carnival

carnival Most people enjoy going to a *carnival* because it is fun entertainment. The original *carnival* was just as fun-filled, but what followed the *carnival* was not! Formed by combining the Latin words, *carne* and *vale*, meaning "Flesh, farewell!" the ancient *carnival* was a three-day festival full of fun and feasting.

carpetbagger During the reign of Queen Victoria (1837-1901), dishonest bankers popularly used luggage made from red carpets. Why? These men would carry their embezzled (stolen) money in this luggage. In time, these crooks came to be called *carpetbaggers*. By the mid-1800s, the meaning of *carpetbagger* expanded to include any unethical person from the northern section of the United States who moved to the southern states (shortly after the end of the Civil War) in hopes of gaining political power by controlling elections. These *carpetbaggers* also sought better business advantages in the northern states. Like the bankers known as *carpetbaggers*, these *carpetbaggers* carried their possessions in a red *carpetbag*. Would the red carpet be rolled out for a *carpetbagger* today?

carpool

Because many items were so scarce and had to be rationed during World War II (1939-1945), Americans were asked to use these items conservatively. This is why *carpooling*, sharing rides and driving, became popular. When the war ended, gasoline was more plentiful, and

"Diamond" carpool lane on a highway

motorists did not *carpool* as much. The oil crisis of the 1970s again forced many to *carpool* (and conserve gasoline). Today, when people drive in a *carpool* lane on the highway, they should drive at a conservative speed.

cashmere

A *cashmere* sweater is always a great gift. Cashmere came from the *Kashmir* (changed to *Cashmere*) region of north India. Who or what provided this wool called *cashmere*? Hairy goats! Now is *cashmere* still at the top of your gift list?

caterpillar

Look closely at a *caterpillar*, and you just might see that it has more hair than you expected. Do not be too surprised! About 600 years ago, the Latin words "*catta*" (cat) and *pilosa* (hair) were combined to accurately name what people saw when they looked at a *caterpillar*—a miniature hairy cat! Now that's a hairy story, Cat!

Caterpillar

cell phone In the 1980s, the cell phone, a hand-held or mobile radio-telephone, became popular with busy businesspeople. Since then, its popularity has certainly grown. This communication device was appropriately named a cell phone because it provided access to a cellular radio network. The cellular phone system is divided into sections or cells, each having its own short-range transmitter/receiver linked to a switching center. Initially a status symbol, the *cell phone* or *cell* quickly became quite useful and, in some instances, a must for many in the fast-paced world of the late 1900s. What would Alexander Graham Bell say about the *cell*?

century The Latin word *"centum"* means 100. Today, a *century* is a period of 100 years. Before taking on its current meaning, a *century* also meant a measure of land, an army of about 100 soldiers, and a unit of 100 prayers. The names of other time periods are also interesting. Ten years is a decade, twenty years is a score, and one thousand years is a millennium. How many *centuries* are in ten millenniums?

Cell phone

century

"The illiterate of the 21st **century** will not be those who cannot read and write, but those who cannot learn, unlearn, and relearn."

—*Alvin Toffler, futurist author*

cheesy (*slang*) Here is an interesting word, for it also means its opposite! In the early 1800s, if you were "the cheese," you were an important person. Perhaps you were so important that you were the "big cheese." In the late 1800s, something called *cheesy* was either ugly or of inferior quality. Why? No one is quite sure! Perhaps it described the quality of some cheese-making processes. Maybe it depicted the look (and smell) of cheese gone bad!

29

By the time *cheesy* entered the youth slang, its meaning had not changed much, for it still meant bad or repugnant. To the 1950s teenagers, one who was *cheesy* was vulgar and lacked taste! The teens of the late 1900s used *cheesy* to mean out of fashion or outdated, as in a *cheesy* outfit. Would you ever call the "*big cheese*" *cheesy*?

chicken feed
(*slang*) It was no secret that the food given to chickens was of poor quality. These inferior wheat and corn grains also had to be small enough for the chickens to swallow them easily. So for the past 200 years, a small amount of money (or change) has been called *chicken feed* because it is not worth much and has little importance. Knowing the history of all the words in this book is no *chicken feed*.

chill
(*slang*) Credit the hippies of the 1960s with this slang word. For them, *chill* meant to "take it easy" or "to relax"—especially when the situation was tense. A few years later, *chill* also meant to refuse to sell drugs to another. Today we like to *chill out* when things are tense or *get hairy*—just like the hippies did years ago. So, the next time you feel pressured, take a *chill*!

coin
Long, long ago, a wedge-shaped tool called a *cuneus* (from Latin) was used to hammer or stamp a design into pieces of metal used as pieces of money. The French adopted the Latin *cuneus* and eventually called it *coing* meaning "wedge." When the English-speaking people finally made the word *coin*, it soon came to mean both the tool and the stamped coin. Just remember that the Latin-speaking people *coined* this word and left their mark on it as well.

Coke
Why is the popular soft drink named *Coke*? Quite simply, the ingredients of the syrup used to make the original *Coke* (or Coca-Cola®) were taken from coca leaves and the Afrikan kola nut. In 1886, Dr. John Stith Pemberton invented the drink in his Atlanta, Georgia drugstore. Pemberton's bookkeeper, Frank M. Robinson, suggested the name "Coca-Cola" since the words name the two ingredients found in the syrup. According to Robinson, the two C's in Coca-Cola, rather than the C from Coca and K from Kola, were better for advertising purposes. It is hard to believe that for more than 100 years people around the world have enjoyed coca leaves and kola nuts! Let's be thankful that *Coke* has other ingredients in it.

Coca-Cola is one of the most popular drinks in the world.

cold shoulder In the early 1800s, a hostess would serve a *cold shoulder* of mutton to guests who had overstayed their welcome. These guests surely "got the message" that they were not wanted there since the meat was both cold and rather unappetizing. Today, one who is given the *cold shoulder* is snubbed or avoided. It is hard to give your best *buddy* the *cold shoulder*.

These commuters are waiting for a train.

commuter For the past 500 or more years, *commute* has meant "to exchange." Since the mid-1600s, *commute* has also meant "to make less severe." It was only in the late 1800s that *commute* meant "to travel regularly to and from work." How then did "to exchange" ever come to mean "to travel to and from work"? Well, rather than buying a railroad ticket each day, one who traveled back and forth from work by train would buy one ticket, at a reduced rate, that would take care of an entire month's worth of travel. So this rider, a *commuter*, both *exchanged* (many tickets for one) and *made less severe* (paid a reduced price). Today, *commuters* do not only ride the train, they take all forms of transportation. Unfortunately, daily traffic jams on expressways and other roads can make *commuting* an unpleasant and stressful experience.

cop (*slang*) Several different stories have been offered to explain the word *cop*. Some believe that *cop* is the shortened form of "copper" since the members of the London police force wore large copper buttons on their uniforms. Others maintain that *cop* was formed by taking the first letter of the three words "*c*onstable *o*n *p*atrol," another term for policeman. Still a third version is that the verb *cop* (as used in the early 1700s), meaning "to capture" or "to catch," was exactly what a policeman did to lawbreakers. Today, the expression "to *cop* a plea" means to plead guilty to a lesser charge. From this probably came the phrase "*cop*-out," meaning "to withdraw" or "drop out." Now do not *cop out* on learning all these stories about *cops*.

Cops

couch potato (*slang*) Staying fit is important to many people but obviously not to everyone! In 1976, a group of Californians, humorously opposing the "get fit and stay fit craze" of that era, preferred vegetating in front of their television sets to doing push-ups, sit-ups, and jogging. Calling himself "a boob tuber" (television sets had sarcastically been called "boob tubes"), one member of this anti-exercise group, knowing that most television watching takes place on the *couch*, went on to substitute *potato* for *tuber*, a synonym for *potato*. So he is the world's unofficial first *couch potato*—and he probably *coined* the phrase from his *couch*!

couch potato

"Drill sergeants say that the decline of mandatory physical education classes in many high schools has contributed to a generation of **couch-potato** teens."

— *Dave Montz in his article, "This Isn't Your Father's Boot Camp Anymore" in USA Today, July 19, 2000, pp.1A-2A*

cracker In the early 1800s, retired Captain Josiah Dent owned a bake shop in Massachusetts. He invented a dough product which he called the "water *biscuit*." Its name was later changed to *cracker* because this crisp *biscuit* made a crackling noise when chewed. A healthy choice for a snack, the *cracker* is all it is *cracked* up to be.

cranberry

The red *cranberry* grows in wetlands and marshes. The old German word for the fruit was *kraanbere*, which means "berry crane." It probably was so named because cranes, the tall wading birds that look like herons, live in the same wetlands. In the mid-1600s, the early Americans were using the German word for these berries, though they spelled it differently. Now you can talk turkey about *cranberry* sauce.

Cranberries

crew

The word *crew* (group of people working together) comes from an old word meaning "to increase." Originally a group of additional soldiers for a military force, this crew of soldiers was used to reinforce or increase the number of soldiers in military units. Later, a ship's personnel (not including the officers), sailboat assistants, and rowing teams were called *crews*. A *crew-cut* was a popular mid-1900s male hairstyle probably first adopted by the boat crews (rowing teams) at two colleges, Harvard and Yale. More recently, a *crew* or a *posse* (primarily an inner-city term) was a group of

friends. *Graffiti* artists who worked together were also called a *crew*. Now you can include the word *crew* in your vocabulary. What an addition!

crib

(*slang*) Today, when people hear the word *crib*, most think of a baby's bed. Yet, more than fifty years ago, Harlem (New York) youth *coined* the word *crib* to mean one's residence. More recently, hip-hoppers and rappers have referred to one's home or apartment as a *crib*. Why would *crib* be an appropriate word for your home?

curfew

Sometimes parents will set a time when their children should be off the streets and back in the house. City authorities often do the same for its residents and visitors in the event of a blackout, rioting, or another cause for possible disturbance. In these instances, a *curfew*, an established time, usually at night, to be off the streets is declared. Almost 700 years ago, French people often unintentionally burned down their thatched-roofed, wooden dwellings because the sparks from their fireplace, a hole built in the middle of their one-room home, would start fires that sometimes destroyed an entire village quite quickly. To minimize the possibilities of such destruction by fire, French city officials enacted a law stating that when a specific bell rang at bedtime, all residents must *couvre feu* (cover/extinguish the fire). The word later became the English word *curfew*. Does this nighttime, fiery story ring a bell? Be back in the house by midnight with your answer...

daisy

Look closely at a *daisy*. Notice that during the day its petals are open and that at night they are closed. For more than 700 years, this flower has been called the "day's eye." Why? Day's eye and *daisy* sound much the same! The *daisy* appears to sleep at night (when the petals close) and to awaken in the morning (when the petals open). Do you think the *daisy* ever oversleeps?

Daisy

dandelion

Nearly 700 years ago, someone who was probably French observed how the leaf of this particular plant looked much like the tooth of a lion. So, the French name *dent de lion*, translated "tooth of a lion," was given to the plant that today is called the *dandelion*. Sink your teeth into that *dandelion* story.

Dandelion

deadline Civil War camps often had a fence, a rail, or a line drawn in the dirt forbidding prisoners to cross that mark. If they did, they could be shot and killed—and often were! Thus, the line became appropriately known as the *deadline*. Today, a *deadline* is the latest time by which something can be completed. Common *deadlines* include those imposed on newspaper reporters and those given to students for their assignments. Luckily, students are not shot if their assignments do not meet the *deadline*.

> deadline
>
> "A goal is a dream with a **deadline**."
> —Napoleon Hill (US businessman and motivational author)

debonair The beginnings of the word *debonair* are up in the air! The falcon, the bird of prey that is trained to hunt and kill, can be ferocious. Yet, some pet falcons, even those that do hunt, are quite tame and graceful. The sixteenth-century French, who loved the sport of falconry, came to admire falcons for the smooth and elegant way they carried themselves. The French said these birds were *de bonne aire* (of good air). Later, the English version, *debonair*, described an "elegant, gracious, well-mannered, and lighthearted" person. Ian Fleming's fictional creation, James Bond, the agent known as 007, is *debonair*. So are many movie stars! And stars, like those falcons, are "of good air."

December On the original calendar, *December* (from the Latin *deca-* for ten) was the tenth month. When Julius Caesar ordered the calendar's change (about 2,000 years ago), *December*, formerly the tenth and currently the twelfth month, retained its original name. The same circumstance applied to the three months prior to *December*. *September*, *October*, and *November*, named for their Latin word origins and positions on the calendar, also kept their names.

dime In the late 1700s, Thomas Jefferson proposed the names "mills, cents, dimes, and dollars" as America's monetary units. Borrowing from the

The head side (left) and tail side (right) of a dime.

French word *dixième* (meaning tenth), he suggested that "our lowest silver coin, ten of which shall be equal to a dollar," be called the *disme* and be pronounced like the word *deem*. Since then, the *s* has been dropped, and the word's pronunciation has been changed to rhyme with *lime*. Yet, through it all, the *dime* is still worth one-tenth of a dollar.

diner Chuck wagons (food wagons that were brought along on the cattle drives of the 1860s and 1870s), local lunch stands, and lunch wagons were some of America's first eateries. These were the ancestors of the modern *diner*. In the 1800s, horse-drawn streetcars were popular in American cities, including New York City, Boston, and Philadelphia. By the turn of the twentieth century, these streetcars had been replaced by electric streetcars. Sensing great opportunity, inventive businessmen converted the antiquated streetcars into lunch cars or diners. These eating establishments did not have great popularity until the enormously successful roadside diners popped up across America in the early 1930s. Today's *diners*, some open twenty-four hours a day, offer both eating convenience and a wide variety of food choices. Care to *dine*?

This diner is shaped like a train's dining car.

dinosaur Though the *dinosaur* is no longer around, its popularity with younger children lives on. The ancient Greeks named the *dinosaur* the "*deinos* (fearful) *sauros*" (lizard). So, the next time you have a nightmare about a *dinosaur* chasing you, just remember that this reptile is, at least to the Greeks of long ago, only a fearful lizard.

One type of dinosaur is this Deinonychus, a meat-eating dinosaur.

dis (*slang*) During the 1980s, the prefix *dis-* from the word *dis*respect actually became a word itself! *Rap* music performers (*rappers*) rapped about people who were *dissin'* (showing disrespect toward) others. Widely used, this three-letter insult was part of the urban youth slang of the time. Even politicians and commentators, certainly major parts of America's mainstream, recognized and used *dis* as a put down! So whether one "talked trash," "ranked on," "tripped on," or "woofed," somebody was insulted or *dissed*. Now show some respect for *dis* because this is the truth about *dis*.

disc jockey According to a 1941 issue of *Variety* magazine, a "*disc jockey* is someone who plays discs (phonograph records) for an audience, on the radio or at a social gathering." Since a horse jockey operates horses, the *disc jockey* or DJ (deejay) operates discs or records. In the early 1980s, video jockeys (*veejays*) were introduced to television viewers on stations such as MTV (Music Television). What will be the next type of jockey associated with the music world?

dog days The ancient Egyptians worshipped *Sothis*, the brightest star in the heavens, as one would worship a goddess. According to the Egyptians, the star's rising flooded the Nile River and made the

probably came from the word "goofy" since they sounded somewhat alike. *Doofus* replaced the 1950s teenage word *square* which also meant one who was "not cool." *Nerd* is the present-day word for this social misfit. Be kind to one labeled *doofus* for you may be working for him or her some day.

doughnuts

Why are these soft pastries called dough*nuts*? The Pilgrims had made these small, solid balls or "nuts" of fried sweetened dough in Holland and then brought the idea to America. And who is responsible for the doughnut with the hole in its middle? No one is quite sure who should be given credit for this. Anyway, the *doughnut*, or *donut* in its shortened form, is still a tasty treat.

Doughnuts

lands fertile. Later, the Greeks called this star *Seirios* (later called the Latin *Sirius*), which meant "scorching" or "burning." In mythology, *Sirius* was also presumably the *dog* of Orion, the famed hunter. Finally, the Romans named this star the "small *dog*" and called the constellation it was a part of the "greater *dog*." So now you know why those uncomfortable, scorching summer days are called *dog days*.

doofus

(*slang*) Plain and simple, a *doofus* is a fool. Like *dip*, this slang word meant loser in the vocabulary of the 1960s teenager. *Doofus*

These people have dreadlocks.

dreadlocks This word for the uncombed, braided hair, characteristic of the Jamaicans, probably originated from fear of the *dreaded* Ethiopian warriors who sported this style of hair. The mere sight of the ferocious warriors' locks of hair would inspire fear in their foes. *Dreds* is the shortened form of *dreadlocks*. Surfer *dudes* probably don't dread the *dreds*, man!

dress down Initially, this term meant to scold or reprimand. A boss could *dress down* a worker for doing a poor job on a project. Then, during the 1990s, American workers took a more casual approach to what they wore to work—at least on one day of the week. The officials in many offices and other work establishments designated a day (usually Friday) to allow workers to wear casual clothes instead of the more formal ones generally worn in the workplace. So rather than having to dress up for work, many took advantage of this opportunity to *dress down*. Would you?

dude

(*slang*) Many think that the surfers of the 1960s coined the word *dude*, but the term really began almost 100 years earlier. At that time a man who was very proper and finicky in both his clothing and manners was called a *dude*. By the 1930s a *dude* was a synonym simply for a guy. When the surfers called each other *dude*, it simply meant a cool guy. The hippies liked *dude* so much that they used it in expressions such as "Hey, *dude*!" just as it is used today. No *dude* is ever a dud! Isn't that a cool idea!

dumbbell

Weight lifters and others who exercise with weights sometimes use a *dumbbell*, the device that has round weights attached to a short bar. A *dumbbell* is usually either lifted or swung about with the hand.

Nowadays, the sound of a bell signifying the time of day or the summons to a church service can be a peaceful and beautiful experience. However, it was not always that way. Perhaps, fortunately, modern-day bells are often rung mechanically or electrically. Long ago, bell ringing was done by hand. Not all bell ringers picked up this skill immediately. Often, the untalented bell ringer's work made for an "unpleasant ear experience." The solution? These less talented ringers would practice with a bell mechanism with silent bells so that no one would hear their mistakes! This *dumb* (meaning silent) *bell* was a welcomed addition to the townspeople who suffered because of these unpleasant sounds. In addition, because those men who rang the *dumbbell* grew strong from swinging and pulling the device, it was also used for weight training. Nowadays, an unintelligent person is also called a *dumbbell* since, like the empty bell mechanism, there is "nothing" in this person's head. Don't ask a *blockhead* about all of this. He probably has no idea.

earmark More than 400 years ago, English farmers slit the ears of their cows as an identification mark. Although this mark was supposed to help prevent the stealing of cattle, thieves often altered the *earmark*—at a bit of a risk. If caught, these thieves could be sent to prison where, as a punishment, *their* ears were slit. Today, an *earmark* is still an identifying mark. As a verb, *earmark* means to set aside for a specific purpose, as "the treasurer *earmarked* that money for the new town park." Have you *earmarked* the derivations of words that you find interesting?

easel The Dutch word for *donkey* is *ezel*. To the Dutch painters of some 400 years ago, a *donkey* and the three-legged frame that artists used to hold the paint canvas while painting were similar. Why? Like the *donkey* that carried equipment, the easel "carried" the artist's canvas during the painting. Some of the artists even felt that the *easel* and *donkey* looked alike. But that's another story for another time.

eavesdropper An *eavesdropper* is one who listens in on the private conversation of others. Why the name? A house's *eave* is the edge of the roof that overhangs the side. Long ago in England, the space of land beneath the *eaves* of a house was called the *eavesdrop* because a person outside the house who wanted to listen in on a private conversation going on inside the house could stand under the house's eaves and *eavesdrop*. Surely, some interesting tidbits were heard by those *eavesdroppers*! Had *Echo* been an *eavesdropper*, would she have *echoed* what she heard?

eavesdrop

"A journalist is basically a chronicler, not an interpreter of events. Where else in society do you have the license to **eavesdrop** on so many different conversations as you have in journalism?"

—Bill Moyers (U.S. newscaster, journalist, commentator, and author)

echo Hera was the Greek queen of the heavens. Her attendant, *Echo*, the daughter of air and earth, was a real talker! One day when *Echo* offended Hera, the queen punished *Echo* by depriving her of all speech except the ability to repeat the words of others. Today an *echo* is the repetition of a sound.

eggnog The American Revolutionary War was a succession of costly, bloody battles during which both the British and the American soldiers fought hard for their respective countries. These soldiers drank a concoction of eggs, milk, sugar, spices, rum, and other spirits. This drink, originally made with a strong ale (*nog*), was introduced to America around 1775 and was appropriately named *eggnog*. Today, *eggnog* is a popular drink during the holiday season. Hopefully, your *eggnog* is not accompanied by any revolutions!

end run The football maneuver called the *end run* features a ball carrier running around one end of the line of players whose team is in possession of the ball. This term was originally called the *end-around* run, but by the early 1900s it was shortened to *end run*. Today, an *end run* also describes any attempt by an individual to bypass (get around) annoying obstacles. The

A glass of eggnog

running back performed an *end run* and gained thirty yards on the play. Later that week, he performed an *end run* when he had his friend, the politician's assistant, speed up his zoning permit.

fan What was the first American sport to have true *fans*? Baseball! The word *fan*, which became part of America's vocabulary in the 1880s, is a shortened form of the word *fanatic*. People who are unreasonably enthusiastic about a sports team are called *fanatics*. They love their baseball and would do almost anything for their team. Team and player *fan* clubs are quite popular with both young and old. *Fan* clubs are not restricted to baseball. There are also fan clubs for rock groups and popular recording artists, to name a few. Now here are a few questions about baseball. How many people do you know who are *sensible* baseball *fans*? How many are baseball *fanatics*?

farce Movies and plays are sometimes called *farces* because they are comedies based on humorous, highly unlikely situations. Often these *farces* include fast-paced, nonsensical action and interesting surprises. Hundreds of years ago, the French theatrical companies would "stuff" or "cram" this humorous play in between the more serious acts of the main theatrical presentation. Why did the French call a *farce* a *farce*? The French word *"farcir"* means "to stuff," and that's no joke!

fast food After World War II, Americans began to move faster. Life in the 1950s and beyond took on a faster pace. Travel had to be *fast*. Service had to be *fast*. So why not *fast* food? Because of the fast-paced lives of many Americans, *fast foods* (some call them *junk foods*), including *hot dogs*, *hamburgers*, *French fries*, and pre-heated dinners, became popular. Nutritional quality was not an issue; it was all about speed. Now there's some junk food for thought.

fast food

"I don't like to eat snails. I prefer **fast food.**"

—*Strange de Jim (French writer)*

fax Starting in the mid-1900s, people were able to send printed material electronically over telephone wires. The transmitted copy of the document, a *facsimile*, Latin for "make alike," could be sent and received within minutes. Shortened forms of the word *facsimiles* have included *facs* and the current *fax*. Today *fax* machines have become an essential part of the business world.

Fax machines work through telephone wires, except that instead of talking to others, you send them a printed message

February As the Roman goddess of fertility, Juno was known as *Februaria*. An ancient custom featured touching an infertile woman with a piece of cloth made from the skins of goats. These goats had been sacrificed to *Februaria*. When touched by this cloth, the woman would be made fertile—thanks to *Februaria*. Thus, the second month of the year was named in *Februaria*'s honor. Originally, *February* had twenty-nine days. That last day, however, was moved to become the last day of *July*, the month named after Julius Caesar. *August*, named after Augustus Caesar, had thirty-one days. So now that both *July* and *August* had the same number of days, thirty, neither Julius Caesar nor Augustus Caesar would feel inferior— or superior.

fender People who escape serious injury while riding in an automobile involved in a crash might thank the car's defender. And what is the car's defender? It is the *fender*, of course, since *fender* is simply the shortened form of defender. Originally, defenders were the names given to the iron cables hung on the sides of sailing vessels to minimize the damage in case of a collision. Interestingly enough, the shortened form of defend is fend (to resist), as in "to fend off an attack." And that is exactly what the car's *fender* does— resists attack.

Ferris wheel

The 1893 World's Fair was held in Chicago, Illinois, and was named the World's Columbian Exposition. The most popular attraction was the *Ferris wheel*. This steel structure, the work of George Washington Gale Ferris, an Illinois railroad and bridge engineer, was 140 feet high, weighed 1,200 tons, and carried 1,440 riders. The popularity of Mr. Ferris's wheel soon spread to many amusement parks around the world. Where is your favorite *Ferris wheel*?

Ferris wheel

"I see nothing in space as promising as the view from a **Ferris wheel**."

—E. B. White (U.S. humorist, essayist, and novelist)

Ferris wheel

flunk (*slang*) *Flunk* initially meant "to fail academically." The word and its meaning entered the American vocabulary in 1823 when a Yale University article contained the expression "*flunk out*." Since then, the word *out* has been dropped, though *flunk* still means to fail academically. It also means to fail in other areas besides the classroom. A *flunk* (or *flunky*) is one who performs simple tasks. Bill Gates probably never *flunked* a computer course! After all, he is no *flunky*!

fortune cookies

For once, boredom paid off! In 1918, David Jung, a Chinese immigrant who owned a noodle company, saw that Chinese restaurant customers looked quite bored while waiting for their food to be cooked and delivered to their tables. The solution? Jung hired a religious minister to write shortened forms of biblical messages to be read by these bored customers. Later, Jung hired a wife of one of his employees to write these fortunes. No longer were these messages or fortunes as religious as those written by the minister. "You shall receive much good luck" and "Your life will be filled with much love," are two messages contained in *fortune cookies*. What message would you like to read in your next *fortune cookie*?

French fries

French fries

If you think *French fried* potatoes were invented in Paris, think again. These *fries* were first made in Belgium in the mid-1800s. Later, their popularity spread to France and then to many other parts of the world. If *French fries* were first made in Belgium, could it be that Belgian waffles were first made in France?

Fortune cookie

Friday Freya, wife of Woden and mother of Thor, was the Norse goddess of love, marriage, and beauty. Woden deserted her when she devoted too much attention to the luxuries in her life—and not enough to him! She might have been the first female to fight for women's rights! *Friday* (Freya's day) is named for this interesting Norse (Norwegian) goddess. The French remember Freya's Roman equal, Venus, in their name for *Friday*, Vendredi.

Frisbee® The workers at the Frisby bakery in Bridgeport, Connecticut, are probably responsible for the plastic throwing disc we today call the *Frisbee*®. For amusement, these bakery employees would throw the aerodynamic tin pie plates during their coffee and lunch breaks. Yale University students in nearby New Haven liked the idea, and they continued the plate-throwing craze that soon spread to many other college

campuses. Registered in 1959 as "Frisbee," the concave plastic dish which spins and is used in catching games has been a popular amusement ever since. People often throw the *Frisbee* in parks, on the beaches, and in neighborhoods. Dogs have even been spotted catching a *Frisbee* though no dog has been spotted throwing a *Frisbee*! Now what would the bakery workers think about that?

Frisbee

funky (*slang*) Thank the French for the slang word *funky*! The French infinitive *funkier* means "to smoke," as one would do with cigarettes, pipes, and cigars. From these tobacco products comes the foul, musty odor of the smoke itself. Thus, in the 1970s and 1980s, *funky* came to mean smelly. Yet, at the same time, *funky* also meant good—in a soulful way, especially in *funky* music. A musician could "play that *funky* music." More recently, rappers used *funky* to mean foul-smelling and disgusting. Lastly, a computer that was acting in a *funky* way did not have a bad smell. Instead, the machine was working erratically.

funny bone There is nothing funny about hurting your *funny bone*, the big bone that runs from your shoulder to your elbow. Then why do we call it the *funny bone*? Simple. The bone's scientific name is the *humerus*, Latin for "upper arm." *Humerus* sounds exactly like *humorous*, a synonym for funny. Now that's nothing to laugh about!

funny bone

"Once you have them by the **funny bone**, their hearts and minds will follow."
—Robert Wieder (journalist and comedian)

49

furlong Over 700 years ago, a *furhlang* was defined as the perfect length of the furrow (narrow groove made by a farmer's plow) in the common field. Over time, *furhlang* became a *furlong*, a unit of distance equal to 220 yards, or one-eighth of a mile. Today, a *furlong* is a standard distance measurement in horse racing. How many *furlongs* make up the Kentucky Derby each spring?

fuzz (*slang*) *Fuzz* as a nickname for a British policeman was used as early as 1915 by the British novelist and playwright Edgar Wallace. In America, *fuzz* was also used in the 1920s by drug dealers and users to designate drug enforcement authorities. Why? Federal narcotics agents of the time were called "Feds" (short for Federals). When these agents raided drug establishments, the lawbreaking dealers and users would whisper, "Feds," to alert the others that the drug enforcement officials were in the building. It is easy to see how a whispered "Feds" could sound much like "*Fuzz*." Today *fuzz*, "cop" (*c*onstable *o*n *p*atrol or the uniform's *cop*per buttons), "pig" (some said that the masks worn by police during riots made them look like pigs), and "5-0" (from the television program *Hawaii 5-0*) are slang words for police.

Equipment of the fuzz

galaxy Would you believe that the word *galaxy* actually means circle of milk? This reference to the Milky Way has been around for more than 600 years. Today, *galaxy* is defined as a system of stars, an assembly of famous people, or a brilliant array of things. Please do not try to count the number of stars in the *galaxy*. Your milk might get sour while you are counting!

This is one part of the Milky Way galaxy as seen from Mount Rainer National Park in Washington State.

gas guzzler During the 1970s American motorists sometimes waited for hours in line in their automobiles to fill their gas tanks. They also saw the price of gasoline and home heating oil rise dramatically. These increases were imposed by-oil exporting countries. Obviously, it was not an advantage to own a large car that "*guzzled*" up gasoline. Why? Owners had to fill their gas tanks with rationed, terribly overpriced gasoline. Owning a *gas guzzler*, called a "gas eater" or "gas hound," could become quite expensive during the Energy Crisis of the 1970s. As a result, many *gas guzzlers* have since been replaced by smaller, more fuel-efficient automobiles.

geek Five hundred years ago a *geek* (or *geck*) was "a loser, a simpleton, or a fool." In the early 1900s, carnival and sideshow performers who swallowed swords or fire were called *geeks*. Then in the 1970s, *geeks* was applied to those unpopular (and often ridiculed) students who spent too much time with their books and too little time at parties. So when the computer craze hit California's Silicon Valley located near San Francisco, these *geeks*, now turned computer *geeks*, built computers and wrote software programs. Today many of these computer *geeks*, now called computer whizzes, like Bill Gates, have become quite popular—and quite rich.

genocide Combining the Greek words *genos* (race) and *cide* (kill) gives us the English word *genocide*. Named by a Duke University professor in 1945, *genocide* described the German leader Adolf Hitler's (and his Nazi

Children in a concentration camp

followers') attempts to physically eliminate the Jewish people during World War II. The Germans used horrific tactics, including torture, concentration camps, and ovens, to kill six million Jewish men, women, and children. In 1948, the United Nations declared *genocide* an international crime. Today, *genocide* is defined as "any act intended to destroy national, ethnic, racial, or religious groups." It is the hope of many that *genocide* will never be attempted again.

genuine

Genero, a Latin word that means "give birth to," is the root of the word *genuine*, which means authentic or real. Later the French used *genu* for knee, as in *genu*flect. In a custom from the olden days, when a father placed a newborn on his knee, he was signifying that he accepted the child as *his* real child. The child was, in essence, *genuine*. So in the father's action, the words *gen*ero (give birth to), *gen* (real), and *genu* (knee) combine to give the word *genuine*. In addition, *Gen*esis is the biblical chapter that recounts the birth of the world. *Gen*iuses are very intelligent from birth. And that's a *genuine* fact.

German measles

Do only German people become infected with German measles (or rubella), the mild, infectious virus disease? Are they the only ones who get the swollen glands and small red spots that accompany this disease? Absolutely not! It is called German measles only because Friedrich Hoffman, a German doctor, was the first to identify it back in 1740. This illness still poses serious health problems, especially for pregnant women. A *German measles* vaccine is a routine childhood immunization.

German measles, or rubella, causes a fever and a rash on the face and neck.

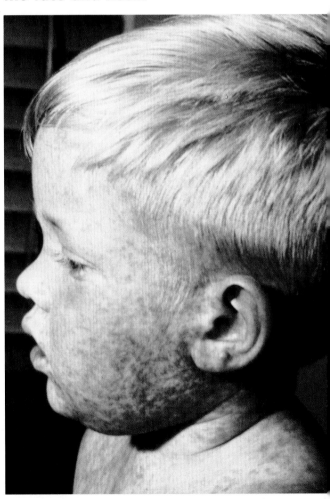

gibberish For the past 400 years rapid, unintelligible talk has been called *gibberish*. The word is probably an imitation of sounds found in nonsense words such as *gibber*, *gabble*, *giggle*, and *jabber*. Remember *gibberish* is foolish and has been for the last four centuries.

gimmick *Gimmick* (a gadget or device for performing a trick) came into American English in the mid-1920s. The men operating the games at the traveling carnivals offered valueless prizes called *gimcracks*. Some of these men cheated the game players by keeping their hand on a *gimmick* that could stop the spinning wheel at a desired spot. So the *gimmick* controlled the number of *gimcracks* that these cheating carnival workers awarded the game players. Today a *gimmick* is anything used to trick somebody. This story is truthful since it contains no *gimmicks*.

glitch (*slang*) Today, a *glitch* refers to a computer malfunction or a problem associated with any mechanical process. Originally a Yiddish (language spoken by Eastern European Jews and their descendants) word for a "slip," a *glitch* was a sudden, brief change in the rotation period of a pulsar (neutron star that gives off radio waves). It is always good to hear that an event, such as the Super Bowl, a king's coronation, or a wedding, went off without a *glitch*.

gnarly (*slang*) The San Fernando *Valley Girls* gave us this word as a synonym for good. Some think *gnarly* might have come from the gnarled roots of the Monterey cypress tree found near the beaches frequented by the *Valley Girls*. So, rather than the more familiar *gnarly* meaning "rough and hardened," the girls' *gnarly* is something quite pleasing. Now isn't that just *gnarly*?

goatee For more than 150 years, we have called the small, pointed beard on a man's chin a *goatee*. Why? The man's *goatee* looks very much like the hair on a billy goat's chin. The word *goatee* actually means "little goat." We know how a man trims his *goatee*. Did you ever wonder how a billy goat trims his chin hair?

This man has a goatee.

goon A person who, unfortunately, is awkward, a bit weird, and stupid is sometimes cruelly referred to as a *goon*. Thank E. C. Segar, the American cartoonist, for this addition to our vocabulary. Segar's comic strip, "Popeye, the Thimble Theatre," included Alice the Goon, a big, stupid creature who appeared in this 1930s comic strip. Did Segar invent this character after the late 1800s slang word *goony* meaning a simple-minded person? Don't ask Alice because she will not know. How would you expect her to know? Remember she—is a goon!

gorilla More than 2,000 years ago, Greek explorers came upon a hairy tribe of West African island women called the *Gorillai*. It seemed natural then to call any hairy, early inhabitant of a region a *gorilla* (the English form of *Gorillai*). In 1847, when Dr. T. S. Savage, an American missionary, first observed the large apes of West Africa, he named them Troglodytes *gorilla*. Luckily, Troglodytes was dropped and today only *gorilla* remains. So hairy tribal women called the *Gorillai* are not your cup of tea, you say?

Gorilla

gourmet It might be hard for some to believe that the French word *groumet*, known today as a *gourmet*, "a person who is a sophisticated judge of fine foods and drinks," was at one time the name for a servant-boy who cleaned and fed horses. *Groumet* later became the name for any minor servant, including the boy who tasted the wine for his wealthy employers. Some of these wine tasters even worked as assistants in wine shops. Eventually, the French *groumet* became the English *gourmet*. Today this expert in wines and fine foods is also called a connoisseur.

graffiti The ancient writings and drawings on the walls of Italian cities were called *graffiti*, the plural of *graffito*. Today, graffiti on walls and other public surfaces (the word is still *graffiti*) can be punishable by law, even though it can sometimes be quite pleasant to the eye. So see the handwriting on the wall, and don't be a *graffiti* artist.

Graffiti on a wall

Graham crackers

In the early 1800s, Sylvester *Graham*, a minister, was ahead of his time in his ideas about health. Preaching how alcoholic drinks, meats, and fatty foods were essentially evil, *Graham* introduced the ideas of eating fruits and vegetables, cutting down on excessive eating, exercising often, and substituting homemade whole wheat flour for white flour. This flour, he believed, had more vitamins and minerals than the white. He was right in all his suggestions! Those who believed in Graham's healthy message named the *Graham cracker* after him. So the next time you eat a *Graham cracker*, think of Minister Sylvester *Graham*.

green room

A television or radio guest relaxes in the *green room* before going on the studio's set. Early in the 1700s, Elizabethan theaters (named after Queen Elizabeth I) had similar rooms called tiring (for attiring or dressing) rooms. Often these rooms were decorated with shrubbery. These green plants were supposed to relax the people waiting to go on stage. Times have changed a bit. Today, though not all *green rooms* are green, some television guests still turn green from nervousness in the *green room*.

Graham crackers

grocer The storekeeper who sells food in great quantities has been called a *grocer* for more than 600 years. England's Company of *Grocers* dealt in large volumes (Latin *grossus*) of spices and produce during the 1300s. Obviously, even though members of England's Company of Grocers do not work in today's supermarkets, our modern-day *grocers* love to sell their items in large quantities.

groggy The next time you feel *groggy* (shaky, dizzy, or sluggish), think of Admiral Edward Vernon, an officer in England's navy in the 1700s. Often seen with his *grogram* coat made of coarse fabric, Vernon earned the nick name "Old *Grog*." Vernon ordered that his sailors' rum be diluted (weakened) with water. Although the seamen were not happy with Old Grog's new order, this less powerful drink, named *grog* after Vernon's attire, could still make them feel *groggy*.

guillotine The *guillotine*, a machine with a sharp blade used to behead people, is often thought of as a cruel death machine. During the French Revolution (late 1700s), capital punishment (death penalty for criminals) took two forms. Commoners were usually hanged, while the nobles were decapitated (beheaded) by a broadax. The ax would not always take the criminal's head off on the first swing. Several swings were sometimes necessary. It was true agony for all involved in the execution! Although he did not invent the machine himself, Dr. Joseph *Guillotin* proposed that a

machine (later named the *guillotine*) be used for a cleaner—and more humane—form of decapitation. So keep your head, and remember how the *guillotine* made some lose theirs.

The blade of the guillotine was very sharp.

gyp Many believe that the gypsies, those wandering groups of people whom the English mistakenly thought came from Egypt, gave us this informal verb meaning to swindle or cheat. In truth, the original gypsies, known for their talents in music and fortune telling, were most probably from India. A *gyp*, from the original word "gippo," is the name of a short jacket that had been worn years ago by the valets (servants) of college students, especially those students attending Oxford, a famous university in Cambridge, England. Since these servants were often cheats and thieves, the word *gyp* became associated with these valets. We hope you do not feel *gypped* with this explanation of *gyp*.

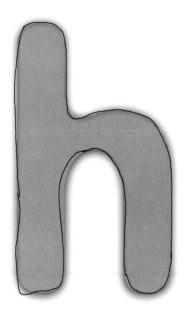

hallmark

Over 700 years ago, English King Edward I ordered the Goldsmiths' Company of London to place its official stamp on all gold and silver items. This stamp would verify the purity (or excellence) of the gold and silver pieces. Thus, these *marks* in the Goldsmiths' Company's *halls* were regarded as marks of excellence. Many greeting card purchasers today feel that *Hallmark* cards continue this tradition of excellence.

hallmark

"The most distinguished **hallmark** of the American society is and always has been change."

—Eric Sevareid (U.S. newscaster)

hamburger

Two different stories about the *hamburger*'s origin have emerged over the years. Geographic locations named *Hamburg* play a part in both histories. Some say that *Hamburg*, Germany, a city known for its chopped meat, gave us the name *hamburger*. Yet, the citizens of *Hamburg*, New York, have a different story. They claim that the first *hamburger* was served in their town. When a concession worker ran out of pork at the town's 1885 summer fair, he used chopped (ground) beef instead. And there, so the New Yorkers contest, is where the *hamburger* originated. The word cheeseburger entered our language in 1938. Interestingly enough, if ham is a type of pork, why does a *hamburger* contain beef and not pork? So, which side of the Atlantic Ocean really gave us the word for that tasty patty of ground beef cushioned within a roll? Bite into that question.

Hamburger

hamstring Long ago the portion of the leg behind the knee was called the ham. The tendon located near the ham was called the *hamstring*. One who rips the *hamstring* usually suffers excruciating pain. So don't be a ham! Do not overwork and injure that *hamstring*.

hard hat (*slang*) Back in the 1880s, *hard hat* was the term used to designate a man, often an Eastern banker or businessman, who wore a derby hat. Almost a century later, *hard hat* designated a construction worker who wore a metal or plastic helmet for protection on the job site. Have you ever seen a picture of a group of *hard hats* eating their lunches as they sit on a building's steel beam more than 50 stories high? It is not hard to tip your hat to these brave construction workers. All hail to these courageous *hard hats*.

Hard hats

haywire Someone or something "gone *haywire*" is disorganized, confused, crazy, or out of order. Farmers used to tie their bales of cut stiff hay with wire. Unfortunately, this wire would often become tangled and caught in the machinery. Sometimes, if the wire was left exposed on the ground, it hurt the farmers, horses, or other livestock that tripped over it. From any (or all) of these malfunctions, the expression "to go *haywire*" was born. People were afraid that many computers would go *haywire* on January 1, 2000. Fortunately, it did not happen.

heavy metal In the late 1970s, *heavy metal* was the term used to describe the very loud, pulsating electronic music of the day. Originally called simply *metal*, *heavy metal* was coined by William Burroughs in his book entitled *Naked Lunch*. Popular heavy metal bands include Iron Maiden, Metallica, and Guns N' Roses.

hero sandwich If the Earl of *Sandwich* is responsible for giving us the word *sandwich*, who gave us the term *hero sandwich*? Was it named after Charles Lindbergh or Babe Ruth—heroes of the early 1900s? Neither! The *hero sandwich* actually started much before these two legends gained their fame. Long ago, men of superhuman strength, courage, and ability were called *heroes*. They were, in a sense, larger than life figures standing far above the rest. So it makes sense that a large-sized sandwich should be called a *hero sandwich*. Depending on where you live, a *hero sandwich* goes by different names. So whether it is called a submarine, a sub, a hoagie, a rocket, or something else, a *hero sandwich* is certainly something big.

hick There are a few versions of how *hick* came to mean one who is an unsophisticated country person.

According to one tale, in the early 1900s, distant rural communities were called *hickory* towns because in those places teachers used the hickory stick to discipline misbehaving students. Shortly after, the people in those rural towns were called *hickories* (from the hickory stick), or simply *hicks*. Another story maintains that *hick* was an altered (changed) form of Richard, the name designating an awkward, simple person living in a rural area. Much like Ichabod Crane in Washington Irving's short story, "The Legend of Sleepy Hollow," Richard, the *hick*, was probably also called a country bumpkin. Some people who live in rural parts are big and strong. It is probably not too smart (or safe) to call them *hicks*.

high seas Those who sailed the ocean waters outside the territorial limits of any single nation sailed what was called the *high seas*. Explorers and other sailors are often associated with the *high seas*. So are pirates. Now whether pirates sailed for booty or adventure, these marauders ventured on the *high seas*. If they sailed during high tides, did they sail the high, *high seas*?

hip (*slang*) In the early 1900s, Americans were using the word *hep* to mean "informed" or "in the know." You were "in the know" if you were *hep*. The musicians of the day told people to "get *hep*" or "get *hep* to the jive." Within a few decades, *hep* was pronounced like *hip*, but its meaning had not changed. Before long, *hip* expanded, and there were *hip*cats, *hip* chicks, and *hip*sters. Then there was *hip*-hop. Today, if you are *hip*, you are cool.

hip-hop (*slang*) Only coined in the late 1970s, the term *hip-hop* is thought to be the product of a Bronx (New York) disc jockey. Seeing the dancers *hip* and *hop* at the parties he worked, the DJ decided to call such affairs *hip-hop* parties. "*Hip-hop*, you don't stop," was his famous line echoed at these parties. Only the *hip* who were *hep* went to the *hip-hop* parties. Are you too *hep* to *hip* and *hop* at the *hip-hop* parties?

hippie (*slang*) Hippies were young people in the 1960s who alienated themselves from the mainstream American culture. Often, these young adults (some *hippies* were a bit older than that) became associated with psychedelic drugs, communal living, innovative trends in rock and roll, and other unusual (for the time) activities. Since these people thought they were *hip* and "with it," *hippie* was an appropriate name. Popular areas inhabited by *hippies* were the Haight-Ashbury section of San Francisco and the East Village of New York City. These were *hip* places for the *hippies*.

A gathering of hippies. The hippie culture valued peace, love, and harmony above all things, and sought to put an end to hatred and violence in the world.

hippopotamus

The ancient Greeks combined *"hippos"* (horse) with *"potamos"* (river) to depict what they thought this animal that spent much time in the water looked like—a river-horse! Please don't expect to see a *hippopotamus* in the Potomac River the next time you visit Washington, DC.

The hippopotamus enjoys spending time above and below water.

hocus-pocus Nearly 400 years ago, when a magician performed his tricks, he used a combination of the words *Hoc* and *est* (*hocus*) from the Latin phrase, *Hoc est corpus meum* (This is my body), used at the Roman Catholic religious service called the mass. Here the priest changes the bread wafer into Christ's body. Similarly, in a sense, the magician also performs "magic." When the magician's *hocus* needed a rhyming word to go along with his trickery, *pocus* fit the bill. Today *hocus-pocus* is still a magician's expression for any form of trickery. Keep your focus and don't fall for another's *hocus-pocus*.

Holocaust Hopefully, the human race will never witness another systematic destruction of a group of people (over 6 million) as the Nazis attempted to do to the Jewish people before and during World War II. This horrendous time in history is referred to as the *Holocaust*. The Bible refers to a *holocaust* as a burnt offering, a type of sacrifice. Though "destruction by fire" is another definition of a *holocaust*, the *Holocaust* of World War II, which did include human burning, is unfortunately the most recognized reference to this word.

homeboy (*slang*) According to the hip-hoppers of the 1970s and 1980s, your *homie*, *homes*, or *Holmes* is your close friend. He is a *homeboy*, and he probably comes from the same neighborhood or *hood* as you. Perhaps the words homie, homes, and *homeboy* originated because this dear friend lives near your home or your *crib*. Could *Holmes* be yet another spelling variation because it refers to the detective, Sherlock *Holmes*, who was Dr. Watson's trusted, close friend? Ask your *homeboy*!

honey Many feel that the colloquial word *honey*, used to designate one's sweetheart or dear one, is an American invention. Interestingly, a gold ring located in the British Museum offers evidence to the contrary. The Greek word *meli* (*honey*) is engraved inside this fourth

Jars of honey

century B.C. piece of jewelry! Since bees produce the sweet substance called *honey*, it seems appropriate that one's sweetheart shares the same name. The Greek who engraved the word *meli* certainly had a *honey* of an idea.

honey

"A drop of **honey** catches more flies than a hogshead of vinegar."

—Traditional Proverb

hood (*slang*) In the language of hip-hoppers of the late 1970s and after, the slang word *hood* meant one's neighborhood or territory. The *hoods* (slang for tough guys) of the 1950s and 1960s had their turf, and the hip-hoppers of the 1980s and after had their *hood*, a shortened form of neighbor*hood*. Many felt right at home "in the *hood*."

hoodlum Several interesting stories concerning the beginnings of the word *hoodlum* have emerged. One of the stories is that *hoodlum* comes from the German word *huddlelump* meaning ragamuffin (a dirty, ragged person). Another even more interesting story comes out of San Francisco in the late 1800s when a notorious gangster named Muldoon terrorized the residents of that California city. For whatever reason, Muldoon's name was spelled Noodlum (Muldoon backwards) by a local reporter. The paper's printer mistook the N for an H, printed it as such, and the word *hoodlum* meaning a wild, lawless person was born. Today hood is a shortened form of *hoodlum*. Neighborhood Watch is a present-day program that protects one's *hood* (neighborhood) from the hoods (*hoodlums*).

hopscotch *Hopscotch* is the children's game in which a player first tosses a flat object into one section of a drawn figure and then hops from one section into another section to pick up the object after each toss. Once called hop-score, the game was not invented in Scotland as its name might suggest. *To scotch* is to score. So when you hop over the lines and pick up the object, you *scotch* or score—the object of *hopscotch*.

hot dog If you are a *fan* (or *fanatic*) of this form of meat often served on a roll, you might not want to hear parts of this story. Some people thought that the shape of the bun and the meat inside it resembled the shape of a dog. And since the meat had been cooked, *hot* was an appropriate word to precede *dog*. Unfortunately, others thought that a *hot dog* was made from meat served to dogs. Not too tasty! Despite all this, a *hot dog* is a popular American food whether it is served at the ballpark, at the mall, in backyards, or on the streets. Which of these two stories about the *hot dog*'s beginning do you relish more?

Hot dog and mustard are a classic combination.

howdy Plain and simple, *howdy* is the shortened form of "How do you do?" The cowboys added partner to *howdy* and so "*Howdy*, partner!" became a familiar phrase in the West. *Howdy* is still used in many parts of the United States.

hulk What do an ancient Greek towed ship and a big, clumsy person have in common? Simple. Both are named *hulk*! From the Greek word meaning "to drag," a *hulk* was an unwieldy ship that was towed behind another sea vessel. Adopted into

English, *hulk* originally meant a large sailing ship before it came to mean the ship's hull (frame or body). Today, *hulk* also means a deserted ship. *The Incredible Hulk*, a popular television show of the 1970s, featured a huge strong monster-like man called, appropriately enough, the Incredible Hulk. *Hulk* Hogan is a wrestler who became popular in the late 1900s. Want some advice? Do not call *Hulk* Hogan big and clumsy. You might regret an encounter with him!

humble pie

If Simple Simon, the pie man, had "to eat *humble pie*," that probably meant he was embarrassed or humiliated because he had to admit a mistake and apologize for it. How did *humble pie* enter the English language? In the 1200s, royal people and rich people ate the good meat, venison, while their lowly, humble servants ate the inner organs or *numbles* (pronounced *umbles*) of the animals. These "*inners*" included the heart, liver, and intestines. Ugh! Thus, *umble* (later changed to *humble*) *pie* was associated with the lower (or humbled) class of people. Would a queen be humbled if she had to eat *humble pie*?

hummer

During the Persian Gulf War in 1991, the U.S. forces employed the *High-Mobility Multipurpose Wheeled Vehicle*. Pronounced "humm-vee," this vehicle, known as the *hummer*, has become a popular land vehicle in the United States. For people who want a rather different means of transportation, the *hummer* is a real *hummer*.

Hummers are gaining popularity in the U. S.

humongous (*slang*) Giants are huge, and *hulks* can be monstrous. Blend *huge* and *monstrous*, and you have *humongous*, a word meaning enormous in size. College and professional football players and wrestlers are often described as *humongous*. The huge, mountainous folk tale character Paul Bunyan is *humongous*. So are whales. *Humongous*—a whale of a word!

husky Believe it or not, a variation of the word *Eskimo* has given us the word *husky*, meaning big and strong. The Eskimos bred these strong arctic dogs used to pull the sleds over long distances in those cold regions, and so explorers named these powerful dogs after the Eskimos themselves. Even today, *husky* designates this particular breed of dog.

hypocrite On stage, an actor or actress pretends to be someone else. Like modern-day performers, *Hypokrites*, an ancient Greek actor, also pretended to be another person. He is probably the most famous pretender or *hypocrite*—at least to the acting world! Today's *hypocrite*, one who pretends to be what he or she is not, is often not trusted by others. Someone who says that he is a health food *fanatic* while eating a large piece of cake is *hypocritical*.

Eskimos like the ones shown here still breed huskies, among other dogs, to pull their sleds. The word *husky* even comes from the word *Eskimo*.

ice cream

ice cream The Italians invented *iced cream* by adding sweeteners and flavorings to cream and then freezing it. In time, this concoction made its way to the American shore. In 1744, the people of Philadelphia dropped the *d* from *iced cream* and enjoyed "some fine *ice cream*" with strawberries and milk. The City of Brotherly Love also invented the *ice cream* soda in 1874. The *ice cream* sundae, which could be eaten on any day of the week, not just on Sunday, came along in the late 1800s. The *ice cream* cone was invented out of necessity (the *ice cream* stand ran out of *ice cream* cups) at the 1904 World's Fair in St. Louis, Missouri. And there's the scoop on *ice cream*.

Ice cream cone

ice cream

"Enjoy your **ice cream** while it's on your plate—that's my philosophy."
—*Thornton Wilder (U.S. playwright and novelist)*

imp Shortened from the Anglo-Saxon word *impian*, an *imp* was originally a graft or a shoot of a plant. Before long, an *imp* became associated with an offspring or child, especially the male child of a noble house. Perhaps because the male offspring, this young demon, behaved as he well pleased, the devilish association of *imp* came into being. That is why today when most of us think of a mischievous child, a little devil, we think of an *imp*. And there is the noble and devilish story of the word *imp*.

infantry *Infantrymen* are those soldiers who go into battle on foot. Although the soldiers in today's *infantry* do ride in trucks and tanks, these modern-day soldiers still spend much of their time on foot—marching. Long ago, the *infantry* derived its name because the Roman soldiers who made up the *infantry* were boy soldiers. One can easily see the word *infant*, meaning baby, in the word *infantry*. This *infanteria*, or infant corps, marched alongside the army officers who rode on horseback into battle. Often these *infantrymen* were also asked to perform under very trying circumstances, including marching in both freezing and extremely hot temperatures. Asked to do such brave tasks, these *infantrymen* probably matured very quickly.

intoxicate DWI (Driving While *Intoxicated* or Driving While Impaired) is a traffic violation. Here *intoxicated*, as it has for the past 400 years, means in a drunken condition, usually from drinking too much alcohol. But *intoxicate* did not always deal exclusively with drinking. The ancient Greek soldiers dipped their *toxons* (bows) into *toxikon* (poison) to poison their arrows—and their enemies. Thus, the Latin *intoxico* meant "to poison." Though *intoxicate* also means "to make wild with excitement or happiness," the association with drinking alcohol, which could be a form of poison, is used much more frequently today.

IOU For almost 400 years, people who lend money to others have required the borrower to sign a note with the three letters *IOU* on it. The three letters simply stand for "I Owe You." Now you owe nothing for this explanation of *IOU*.

Ivy League

Today the term *Ivy League* means the best, first-rate, or first-class. You might have an *Ivy League* smile or *Ivy League* intelligence. In the 1930s, a sportswriter wrote of the eight highly regarded Eastern colleges that made up one of the football conferences. These eight schools, Brown, Columbia, Cornell, Dartmouth, Harvard, Pennsylvania, Princeton, and Yale, were well known for their academic reputations—and their *ivy*-covered buildings! These colleges are still considered to be some of the finest schools in the world—with or without their *ivy*-covered buildings.

Princeton University—an Ivy League school

jacuzzi Whether a *jacuzzi* is used for therapeutic or leisure purposes, this bath featuring underwater jets of warm water was originally made to help improve painful ailments such as arthritis. The original *jacuzzi* of the 1950s, invented by the *Jacuzzi* brothers, was a portable whirlpool pump placed free-standing in the bathtub. It pushed jets of warm water into the bathtub. By 1968 the whirlpool bath came into existence, followed several years later by the whirlpool spa. Today, in addition to its medicinal uses, the *jacuzzi* is used by health club members who enjoy the pleasures of this whirlpool bath. *Jacuzzis* are even found in many homes. Maybe that is why they say, "There is no place like home."

January The Roman god, Janus, was the gatekeeper of the heavens. His name is taken from the Latin word for "door." Janus supposedly had two faces—one looked back at the past year, and the other one looked toward the future.

The story behind the month of *January* is an interesting one. The oldest Roman calendar had only ten months. The calendar year began in *March* and ended in *December*. The months of *January* and *February* did not exist. They were only added about 2,700 years ago. *January* was so named because a feast day dedicated to Janus was celebrated during that month. When the Julian calendar, named in honor of Julius Caesar, was adopted (a little more than 2,000 years ago), the beginning of the year was moved to *January* 1.

Ironically, it was not until the late 1500s that many of the world's countries accepted January as the year's first month. England and its colonies waited until the mid-1700s before they adopted this idea. Whew! Since Janus was also known as the god of beginnings, *January*, the first month, the year's beginning, seems to be an appropriate name.

January

"Sharks are as tough as those football fans who take their shirts off during games in **January**, only more intelligent."

—Dave Barry (U.S. columnist and humorist)

Jeans hanging on a clothesline

jeans

Many years ago, a strong, twilled cotton cloth was made in the Italian city of Genoa. The name of this cloth was originally Gene fustian, combining Gene (a form of Genoa) and fustian (cloth made from cotton, flax, or wool). In time, fustian was dropped, and either Gene or Jean was used to designate the name of this cloth. It was not until the mid-1800s that *jeans* was recorded as a plural noun. Blue *jeans* are a popular form of this cloth that is used today for both work and casual wear. The famous explorer Christopher Columbus lived in Genoa. Do you think he wore blue *jeans* as he sailed the ocean blue on his way to America?

jeans

"[Blue **jeans** are] the most beautiful things since the gondola."
—Diana Vreeland (U.S. fashion editor)

jeep You have probably seen many vehicles called *jeeps* on the road. The word *jeep* has at least three possible origins. In the 1930s, the U.S. Army designated this type of motor vehicle *G.P.* (*General Purpose*), which sounds much like *jeep*, right? Around the same time, in the *Popeye* comic strip, a character named Eugene the *Jeep* constantly cried "*jeep, jeep!*" Some have even suggested that *Jeep* came from "Jeepers creepers!"—the remark of riders upon their first ride in the G.P. vehicle. Well, jeepers creepers, what is the *jeep*'s real story?

Jeep

jelly Most people do not freeze *jelly*. They merely refrigerate it. Originally, *jellies* were frozen desserts. The Latin word *gelata*, meaning "to freeze or solidify by freezing," helped give the original frozen dessert (*jelly*) its name. Long ago, the Romans made *jellies* by boiling animal bones. This liquid then cooled and solidified. And, legend has it, this process then suggested freezing the solid mixture. Anyone for *jelly* spiced with some animal bones?

Jelly

jeopardy Thank the French for this word meaning great danger. "*Jeu parti*" (a term that sounds like *jeopardy*) was a chess term meaning "a divided game, or a game with even chance." By the late 1300s, the *jeuparti* (now one word), meant any danger or risk. Within another 200 years, the English spelling, *jeopardy*, was adopted. Do you feel any danger when you watch the game show *Jeopardy*?

jinx Over 1,000 years ago, the southeastern U.S. bird called the *jynx* supposedly had the ability to predict the future. Some people would actually trust this bird to tell them their fortunes! Too often, the *jynx*'s favorable predictions did not come true. Unfortunately, too many of the bird's unfavorable predictions came true! In time, this black magic bird's name became forever associated with bad luck. Today, *jinx* means "any person or thing supposed to bring bad luck" or "a spell of bad luck." Should we put a *jinx* on the *jynx*?

jive (*slang*) In the early 1920s, the blacks of Chicago would playfully (or sometimes sarcastically) insult one another. Initially, this insulting was called "putting you in the dozens." It later became known as *jiving*. By the 1930s, *jive*, probably an offshoot of *gibe* or *jibe* ("to playfully tease"), found its way into the world of Harlem (New York) and Chicago jazz where it was known as the "playful improvising with the melody." Over the years, *jive* has meant "to kid or talk insincerely" as in, "Are you jiving me?" The hippies of the 1960s also used *jive* to mean "deceptive talk or nonsense." Lastly, from about the late 1930s to the 1960s, *jive* was a synonym for marijuana. A marijuana cigarette was a *jive* stick. There is no *jiving* in this story about *jive*.

July

July was originally named *Quintilis* (Latin for fifth). At that time, the calendar began with March, and *July* was the fifth month. *Julius* Caesar was a Roman general and statesman born during this month. The Roman senate renamed this month in honor of *Julius*. What we now call *July* in English came into wide use the same year that Julius Caesar was assassinated: 44 B.C.

June

Some say that June is named after Juno, and others say after Junius. Juno was the queen of the Roman gods and the goddess of marriage. In early Rome, many marriages took place in *June*. The *June* wedding tradition continues even today. Junius was the name of a prominent ancient Roman family. One of the family members, Lucius Junius Brutus, was elected Rome's first consul (one who administers the law). This same Junius family was responsible for Julius Caesar's assassination. Either the entire family or simply the consul himself was honored through the name *June*. Juno or Junius? The debate rages on!

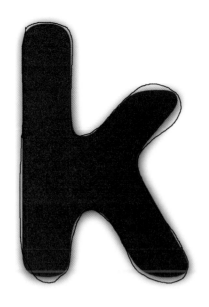

kidnap During the 1600s and 1700s, the new land called America was in need of cheap labor. There were not enough servants and slaves to do all the necessary work such as clearing land and building roads. At the same time, most London families were often financially hard pressed, and, as a result, their children learned to fend for themselves in the London streets. Looking to use these poor children as laborers in America, some opportunists would convince the children that life in America would be wonderful. Even if the children chose not to go to America, these people would force them and load them onto the cargo boats along with the other children. The conditions were so intolerable that some of the children died or became quite sick on their voyage to America. Upon landing in the new country, these children were sold to those needing their services. This child stealing, known as *kidnapping*, came from the words *kid* (child) and *napping* (stealing). A famous kidnapping (1932) involved the child of the heroic American aviator, Charles Lindbergh, the man who flew solo from New York to Paris in 1927.

killie How could the *killie*, the little, innocent fish that we use for bait, have a name associated with murder. Well, *killie* is the shortened form of killfish, a word formed from the Dutch *kille* (channel or stream) and *visch* (fish). These *killies* do involve themselves in murder since they control the mosquito population by eating these insects. Now there's some food for bait—and thought.

knot Land speed is measured in miles per hour, and water speed is measured in *knots* per hour. A ship that has traveled 600 *knots* has traveled 700 miles since a knot (6,076 feet) is longer than a mile (5,280 feet). Why is water speed measured in *knots*? For hundreds of years, the line thrown overboard to measure a ship's speed was marked off in *knots*. Mariners could tell the boat's speed by the number of *knots*. So, is *knot* not an appropriate word to use to measure sea speed?

ladybug

After counting the number of black spots on the *ladybug*, have you ever wondered why this beetle is called a *ladybug*? Named after the Blessed Virgin (Our Lady), the *ladybug*, like the mother of Jesus, helps others. The *ladybug* feeds chiefly on insect pests and their eggs—a real help to gardeners. Bugs should beware of the *ladybug*.

lame duck

Nearly 150 years ago in England, a *lame duck* was one who lost so much money on the stock market that he could no longer meet his financial obligations. Obviously, this person was weakened, or lame, since he most often could not make a move financially. The expression *lame duck* came into American politics in the mid-1800s. It referred to an

Ladybugs

official who had been defeated for reelection and had to complete the rest of the term. Much like the earlier *lame duck*, this *lame duck* was crippled (politically) since he most often could not perform important political actions. The ousted official's term would end shortly so the *lame duck* just sat there until the new official took over. How many *lame ducks* will there be after the next election?

left-handed compliment

During the Middle Ages (476-1450) in Germany, and later in some other countries, if a member of the royalty married a commoner, a special ceremony, including some interesting arrangements, took place. It was agreed that neither the commoner nor her children would have a claim on the royal groom's title or property. All the wife would receive was a gift for the morning after the wedding night. Equally interesting was the fact that during the ceremony itself the groom gave his left hand instead of the customary right hand to the bride when exchanging the wedding vows. This soon became known as a *left-handed compliment*, an insult that is disguised as a compliment.

leotard
Jules Leotard was a French trapeze artist of the mid-1800s. He designed his own costume, a one-piece, tight-fitting suit, so that he could easily perform his aerial maneuvers. Today, almost a century and a half after Leotard designed this costume, it is still called a *leotard*. Leotard's garment is also worn by dancers, acrobats, and gymnasts. Assuredly, Leotard would fly through the air with the greatest of ease (in his *leotard*) if he knew that today his name is known around the world.

This woman is wearing a leotard.

limerick This nonsensical, humorous poem of five lines, whose first, second, and fifth lines rhyme (as do its third and fourth lines), was a form of poetry popularized by Edward Lear in the 1800s. How a *limerick* became a *limerick* is debatable. Some believe that the word Learic (name given to Lear's poetic form) died a rapid death and was later replaced by the word *limerick*, inspired by a song's chorus about "coming up to *Limerick* (Ireland)," sung after each verse at parties. Anyway, "There once was a poem called a *limerick*... Whose beginnings were dark and thick...."

limey (*slang*) In the late 1700s, British navy men used lime juice as protection against a disease called scurvy. Some fifty years later, the Australians were calling the British sailors and their ships *lime-juicers*. This was later shortened to *limeys*. Although the word *limey* was somewhat of an insult in those days, today it refers affectionately to any Englishman. Long live the *limey* lads and lassies of London.

Drinking the juice from the lime gave British navy men the nickname *limey* during the 1700s. Today, it is a friendly term for any Englishman.

Lindy Do you like to dance? The waltz, the can-can, the limbo, the twist, and the electric slide have been popular dances in their times. But have you ever heard of the *Lindy*, a popular American dance from the late 1920s to the mid-1950s? This jitterbug dance was named in honor of Charles Lindbergh, the American aviator and hero, the first person to fly solo across the Atlantic Ocean. Lucky *Lindy* flew nonstop from New York to Paris in 33 hours in 1927! Would you have liked to *Lindy* in New York or Paris with a true American hero?

links It could easily be assumed that golf *links* are so named because the holes are linked together by number (1-18). Actually, *links* became the name because many Scottish golf courses were originally built along the seashore on *hlincs* (slopes or ridges of land). St. Andrews in Scotland and Pebble Beach in California are two famous golf *links*.

lollapalooza (*slang*) Since the 1920s, the slang word *lollapalooza* has meant anyone or anything very striking, extraordinary, or exceptional. How the word originated is debatable. Some say that it started with the *lulu appaloosa*, a huge flathead catfish. Because of its size, this fish was certainly a *lollapalooza*! Others believe that *lollapalooza* might have begun as

an offshoot of the French term *allez-fusil* (meaning "forward the muskets"), supposedly spoken by the French forces but incorrectly heard by those who thought the French said something more akin to *lollapalooza*. Since no one is certain of the word's origin, make up your own *lollapalooza* of a story.

long johns We can thank Friedrich Ludwig Jahn, a nineteenth-century German gymnastics teacher, for coming up with this term for the long underwear that usually covers the legs to the ankles. Jahn contributed heavily to the sport of gymnastics, inventing the horizontal bars, the parallel bars, the side horse, and the balance beam. In addition, he introduced a tight-fitting, full-body exercise suit that was appropriately called the "long Jahn." By the time this outfit made it to America's West, the settlers and miners who wore this clothing as an undergarment called it *long johns*. And that's a short history of *long johns*.

lord Would you ever think that at one time a British *lord* was in charge of guarding the bread? Well, that's exactly what the word *lord* means— "guardian of the bread or loaf." Since bread was, and still is, a needed food, the person who guarded the dough had an important position. Though a lady, by definition, was one who "kneaded the bread," the *lord* was one who both guarded the bread and ruled his household. Over the years, a *lord* has come to signify a man of authority both in one's domain and in society. In England, *lords* are noblemen—either by birth or by special courtesy of the British crown. Today's wealthy *lords* certainly have more than enough bread to eat and to spend! They can afford hiring someone else to guard the bread—and the estate.

love

We can trace *love* meaning "zero in tennis" to the French. Its origin is really quite simple and logical. The French word for egg is "*l'oeuf*." An egg has the same shape as a zero.

"*L'oeuf*" is pronounced much like *love*. So in today's tennis, a goose egg (or a score of zero) is *love*! Tennis, anyone?

lunatic

Many of us today are struck by the moon's beauty. However, if you were living about 700 years ago and were "moonstruck," you would have been called a *lunatic*, a word that today refers to insane behavior. Supposedly, Luna, the mythological Roman moon goddess, caused people to become mad or crazy by changing the phases or cycles of the moon. It was believed that as the moon became fuller, those under Luna's (and the moon's) influence would become crazier and more violent. This "moon madness" is still in our vocabulary today.

People once believed that the moon caused lunacy.

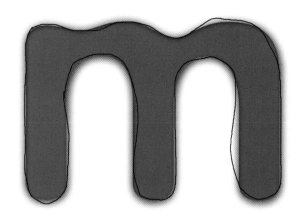

magazine

magazine The Arabic word for a place where grains and other supplies are kept is *makhzan*. Borrowing from the Arabian language, English speakers gave the name *magazines* to books because books are truly storehouses of knowledge. In the 1800s, the word *magazine* no longer applied to books only. Instead, periodicals (published at regular intervals of more than one day) were called *magazines*. It is the same today. *Time*, *Newsweek*, and *Sports Illustrated* are current popular *magazines*.

malaria Those who live in Buenos Aires, Argentina, supposedly have "good air" since that is exactly what Buenos Aires means. The Italians of more than two centuries ago were not as fortunate. They believed that the bad air or *mala aria* near swamps and marshes caused a disease accompanied by severe chills and fevers. Even though it was later discovered that the anopheles mosquito, and not the bad air, caused this disease, the name *malaria* remains to this day.

marathon The battle of *Marathon* was fought about 2,500 years ago between the Athenians and the Persians. Although the Athenians were greatly outnumbered, they still won the battle and defended their homeland. Following the battle, Pheidippides, an Athenian soldier, ran to Athens, about 25 miles from *Marathon*, to announce the Athenian victory. As he arrived, he shouted, "Nike!" ("Victory!"). He then collapsed and died from exhaustion.

The New York City Marathon

The *marathon* became a racing event in the modern Olympic Games when these athletic contests were started in Athens, Greece, in 1896. (The first Olympic *marathon* was even won by a Greek runner.) Twelve years later, the Olympics were held in London, England. Race organizers wanted the queen of England to see the end of the race from her box in the London stadium. So they extended the *marathon*'s distance to 26.2 miles and placed the finish line in front of the royal box.

Today this premiere foot race is one of the main events at the Summer Olympics. Other popular *marathons* are held in New York City, Boston, Chicago, Los Angeles, London, and other cities. In some of these *marathons*, as many as 25,000 runners compete for the prize. Because it takes such great effort to run a *marathon*, the word *marathon* can also be used to describe any activity requiring stamina and endurance. If you read this book in one *marathon* sitting, you are likely to be tired.

March Before Julius Caesar's reign as dictator of the Roman Empire (over 2,000 years ago), the calendar began with *March*, a month named after Mars. The ancient Romans believed that Mars was the god of agriculture who then became the god of war. Thinking that this month was a good month to make sacrifices to this agriculture god for a successful crop that year, they named it *March*—after Mars. The later Romans believed that *March* was an appropriate name for the month since this period was an opportune time to start waging wars. So Mars, in his capacity as god of war, was duly honored by them. Whether he is remembered through agriculture or through war, Mars is honored in *March*.

Mardi Gras Lent, the Christian forty-day period of prayer, fasting, and abstaining (giving up certain pleasures), begins on Ash *Wednesday* and ends on Easter *Sunday*. The English-speaking world calls the *Tuesday* immediately before Ash *Wednesday* "Fat *Tuesday*." The French equivalent of Fat *Tuesday* is *Mardi Gras*. So, *Mardi Gras* is the last day to get fat because almost seven weeks of doing without many pleasures follows. After *Mardi Gras*, the carnival ends, and fasting begins.

Vibrant colors decorate New Orleans for the celebration of Mardi Gras.

margarine The next time you think of substituting *margarine* for butter, remember the following story. The English word *margarine* is from the Latin *margarita* (pearl). Before dyes were added, *margarine* was white and pearly-looking. You might not want to know this, but *margarine* was extracted (taken from) hog's lard (fat). *Margarine*...a tasty pearl of a story.

Martian If you are familiar with the Roman gods and goddesses, you probably know that Mars was the Roman god of war. Mars gave his name to Tuesday, the planet Mars, the month of *March*, and the martial arts (such as karate and judo)—to name a few. In literature known as science-fiction, a *Martian* is a creature from Mars. For those who claim to have seen a UFO, an unidentifiable flying object, they might have also witnessed a *Martian* invasion! So truly where did the word *Martian* originate? Some people favor the god Mars (who was Roman). Others prefer the *Martians* from outer space (who enjoy roamin'). Hey, let's not fight about it!

maverick Cattle owners usually brand their cattle (place a mark on them with a hot iron) for easy identification. In the mid-1800s, Texas cattle owner Samuel Maverick did not follow the branding practice of the other owners. These unbranded cattle that did not go along with the rest of the herd members were known as Maverick's (cattle). Today, a *maverick* is a nonconformist who does not go along with the crowd. Do you go along with this story or are you a *maverick*?

May A bit of uncertainty surrounds the history of *May*. This month is probably named after *Maia*, the Greek earth goddess of spring and the mother of Mercury. *Maia* is thought to be responsible for the continuing growth of the spring crops. Flowers look quite beautiful during *Maia's* month, the merry month of *May*.

Mayday The international radiotelephone signal for help used by ships and aircraft in distress is called *Mayday*. This *Mayday* has nothing to do with the other May Day, the spring festival celebrated by dancing around a maypole and crowning a May queen on the first of May. Instead, thank the French for this distress word since the French words (*venez*) *m'aider* mean "(come) help me"—an appropriate plea from one in trouble on the water or in the air.

mayonnaise This creamy salad dressing or sauce is made by beating together egg yolks, olive oil or other vegetable oil, lemon juice or vinegar, and seasoning. This was an invention of the Duc de Richelieu's chef to honor the Duc after he captured *Mahon*, a seaport on the island of Minorca, an island east of Majorca. The *mahonnaise* made by the Duc's chef is now spelled *mayonnaise* and is a popular addition to sandwiches and salads. Do you wonder if a chef's salad contains *mayonnaise*? It is truly a tasty issue.

Jar of mayonnaise

melting pot Quite often, the United States is referred to as a "*melting pot*" because those who have immigrated from various nations have become a part of America's main cultural body. These immigrants have "*melted* in." The immersion also includes different races, religions, and more. Today, America is also referred to as a "salad bowl." As in the past, different types of people have come to America and "*melted* in" with the others. But today, immigrants have made a greater effort to retain their former identity, be it race, religion, or ethnicity. So, like the items in a salad bowl, they are mixed with others, yet they are still unique. When did your ancestors become part of America's *melting pot*?

mess Ever wonder why the area where army soldiers eat together is called the *mess* hall? Is it because they leave it a *mess*? Certainly not! The word *mess* is taken from the French word *mes* for a prepared food dish, especially a liquid food, such as broth or porridge. So when this quantity of food and the place where it is consumed are joined in the same term, a *mess* hall seems to be an appropriate name for this room. Three hundred years ago, the writer, Alexander Pope, used the word *mess* for the liquid or mixed food given to animals. Perhaps because this food concoction looked so awful, the word *mess* for a concoction or jumble became part of our language. Nearly 100 years later, *mess*, meaning a state of confusion, was first recorded. Now that's the dirt on the word *mess*.

migraine

The person who suffers from *migraine* headaches might feel as though his head is about to split wide open. Actually, since this type of headache attacks "one-half the head," the word *migraine*, formed from the ancient words meaning "half" and "skull," seems to be an appropriate name. And that's not a half-bad explanation of the *migraine*.

Bed rest and an ice pack are helpful in treating a migraine.

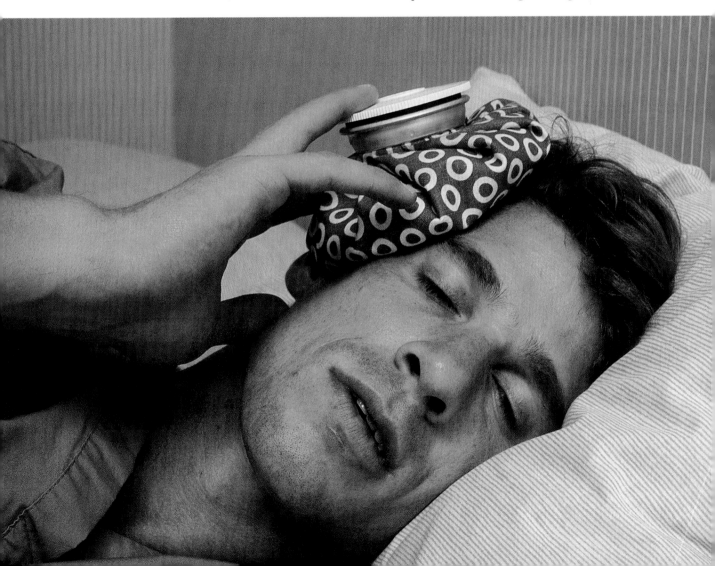

milestone Augustus, the first Roman emperor, ordered a stone called a *milliarium* to be placed in the center of the Forum, the public square of ancient Rome. From this stone, whose name meant "a thousand," all distances would be measured. The Roman mile was the equivalent of a thousand paces. Each pace was approximately five feet. A milliarium was placed at every thousandth pace mark along these ancient Roman roads. From this, we adopted the idea of marking our roads at every mile, though we usually use signs instead of stones. So in today's vocabulary, a *milestone* is a stone or pillar set up to indicate distance. It is also a significant event, especially in history or in a person's life. What are some of your personal *milestones*?

milestone

"Life isn't a matter of **milestones**, but of moments."

—Rose Kennedy (Mother of a U.S. President and U.S. author)

modem During the 1950s the computer world gave us the word for this device that connects a computer to a telephone or cable. *Modem* is a combination of the words *modulator* and *demodulator*. To *modulate* means to vary the intensity and frequency of a wave in accordance with some signal. To *demodulate* essentially means to detect or recover the wave at the receiver. Thus, a *modem* converts data to a form that can be transmitted to data-processing equipment where a similar device reconverts it. A computer's *modem* can be internal (inside the computer) or external (outside the computer). *Modem* is a rather modern word.

Monday In mythology, the moon was supposedly the sun's wife. Since *Sunday* was the sun's day, *Monday* was named after his wife, the moon. Through the years, the moon has been associated with various superstitions, including lunacy and odd behavior. Do many people become moonstruck on *Mondays*?

monster We all know that a *monster* is a real or imaginary creature that horrifies us. Mary Shelley's *Frankenstein* and Bram Stoker's *Dracula* are famous, fictional scary *monsters*. Cookie *Monster* is not as threatening (unless he is denied his cookies)! Today, the slang word *monster* is something quite different, for it refers to something remarkably successful or outstanding. Michael

Actor Boris Karloff as Frankenstein's monster

Jordan's *monster* career as a professional basketball player is legendary. There are *monster* salaries, *monster* contracts, and *monster* waves. What *monster* achievements are in your future?

moose Almost 400 years ago, the Abenakis (Indians living mainly in Maine and south Quebec) gave us the word *moose*, which means "he trims or cuts off," referring to how the *moose* eats bark and twigs off trees. Do you think a *moose* would bark up (or eat up) the wrong tree?

moron At their 1910 convention, the American Association for the Study of the Feeble Minded adopted a word to describe the type of patients they worked with each day. This type of patient was mentally retarded or well below normal intelligence. *Moron* owes its beginnings to two sources. The group was reminded that the French playwright, Molière, had created *Moron*, a very simple-minded individual. *Moron* was much like the patients they knew. Then using the Greek word *moros* (foolish), the group decided to name such a person a *moron*. It is interesting that *moron* is one of the few words voted into the English language. That's not too foolish!

Morse Code

In 1844, Samuel Morse invented the *Morse Code*, a code that sent messages and signals by telegraph. The system consists of dots and dashes (or short and long sounds or flashes) that represent letters, numbers, and punctuation. Interestingly enough, Morse was a painter and sculptor after he graduated from Yale University, a Connecticut *Ivy League* school. "What hath God wrought" were the words of Morse's first successful *Morse Code* message. Do you want to send your own *Morse Code* message? Just add a dot of this and a dash of that.

Motown

Detroit, Michigan, is a world-leading producer of automobiles. It has often been referred to as the Motor City. In the early 1960s, Berry Gordy, Jr. started a record label named *Motown* (short for Motor City). Since then, *Motown* has been a leading producer of hit music. Sing along (and drive) in *Motown*!

Panoramic view of the skyline of Detroit, the Motor City or *Motown* as it is sometimes called, at night

mouse The often-undesirable, small rodent called a *mouse* sometimes frightens people and causes them to shriek, "Eek, a *mouse!*" The small, hand-held computer device, named the *mouse* in the 1960s, is a necessity if you want to operate a computer's cursor. Because the *mouse* is moved as it is and because the *mouse*'s cord resembles the rodent's tail, the name *mouse* is an appropriate name for this computer accessory. Now let's move on and high-tail it out of here!

Which type of mouse would you rather have near your computer?

mush French trappers (those who trapped fur-bearing animals for their skins) in America's Northwest helped add this word to the English language. These trappers would often shout, "*Marchons!*" (French for let's go" or "move faster") to their sled dogs that pulled them through the snow. "*Marchons*" eventually became "Mush on" in English before it finally became "*Mush!*" If you have to *mush* through the snow to get to school, remember the trappers had it much (or *mush?*) easier. They had dogs to move them along.

Napoleon

Have you ever enjoyed a *napoleon*, the delicious, rectangular layered pastry with custard filling? Many people are under the misconception that the pastry was named in honor of Napoleon, the French emperor of the early 1800s. Not true! Because these tasty treats were first made in Naples, Italy, they were appropriately named Napolitain, which through a mispronunciation or two eventually became *napoleon*. Would Napoleon have enjoyed the taste of a *napoleon*? "Undoubtedly!" say the people from Naples.

Contrary to what many believe, the napoleon pastry is not named after this man, the Emperor Napoleon Bonaparte.

nausea Although the French call it *mal de mer*, the Greeks were the originators of *nausea*, the modern-day word for seasickness. The Greek words *naus* (ship) and *nautes* (sailor) were the inspirations for the word used today to describe the stomach disturbances experienced by sailors on the seas. Today *nausea*, though it ends with the word *sea*, is not confined to the sea. A person experiences *nausea* when he is sick and feels the urge to vomit. Travelers who have a tendency to become nauseous often take preventive measures, perhaps a pill, to avoid *nausea*. You and the sailors around the world probably feel better now that you know *nausea*'s history.

Some pills help people avoid nausea

NIMBY An acronym (a word formed from the first letters of a word or words) for *Not In My Back Yard*, *NIMBY* refers to those people who object to certain other people and things in their neighborhood or immediate surroundings. A *NIMBY* often protests against landfills, waste disposals, prisons, factories, malls, and other "undesirable" facilities placed in his area. A *NIMBY* who detests the fact that "less desirable" people might move into his neighborhood can also be heard to say, "*Not In My Back Yard!*"

November The Latin *"novem-"* (nine) is the basis for the name *November*, originally the ninth calendar month. In 45 B.C. (Before Christ), when the calendar was changed under Julius Caesar's direction, *November* became the eleventh month. Even though *November*'s place on the calendar changed, the name, probably for convenience sake, stayed the same.

nuke (*slang*) This word meaning "to attack with nuclear weapons" is a shortened form of the word nuclear. We hope we never hear that a country was *nuked* by another. Of course, people also *nuke* food in their microwaves. This nuking is convenient because it saves time. Care to *nuke* some popcorn tonight?

Popcorn can be *nuked* in a microwave.

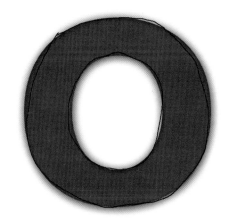

October

This month was originally the eighth calendar month. Since "*octo-*" is the Latin prefix for eight, the name fits well. When the calendar was changed (45 B.C.), and *January* began the year, *October*, now the tenth month, did not undergo a name change. Since Halloween concludes the month of *October*, children love the end of this tenth month.

Orient

It is very appropriate that Japan, a country in the *Orient*, is called the Land of the Rising Sun since the sun rises in the East, the *Orient*, and sets in the West, the Occident. Very simply, *Orient* means "rising," and Occident means "falling" or "setting." Long ago many superstitious people associated good luck with the *Orient* and bad luck with the Occident, for the sun's rising represented new life and the sun's setting represented the end of life. Hope you got a rise out of this story about the *Orient*!

Ouija® board

Those who believe in spirits may use a *Ouija® board* to spell out messages and hopefully answer questions about life.

Ouija board

Combining "*oui*" (French for *yes*) and "*ja*" (German for yes), the *Ouija board* is supposed to give "yes" answers (*oui-ja*!) to these questions. Do some people today still trust the *Ouija board* for life's answers? *Oui! Ja!*

outrageous *(slang)* "How outrageous!" How often have you heard this expression? Does the speaker mean the intolerable *outrageous*, "that which exceeds all bounds of what is morally decent" (like an insult) or *outrageous* in the sense of "that which means excellent" (like a surfer's great wave)? The French *outre* and the Latin *ultra* (both meaning *beyond*) have

helped to give *outrageous* its meaning. To the hippies, *outrageous* meant something really terrific, in the same way that *dynamite* or *primo* did! Years later, *outrageous* continued to mean excellent! *Outrageous* is certainly an *outrageous* word.

outrageous

"In difficult times fashion is always **outrageous**."

—*Elsa Schiaparelli (Italian-French designer)*

page If you are *paged* at a restaurant or other establishment through an intercom, electrical device, a person, or other means, you might be reminded of the olden-day boy-servant, called a *page*, who lived in England one thousand years ago. A *page* performed everyday humble tasks, including running errands and carrying messages, for his wealthy, important employer. Thus, when this *page* went to a public place to search for a person, he would "*page*" the requested individual. And there's a *page* out of that boy-servant's story.

Electrical devices like this headset are now used to page people in public.

pan out When a situation *pans out*, it works out well. Gold miners "*panning* for gold" used a pan, a shallow circular metal vessel, to wash gold from gravel. If the miner found gold in his *pan*, his effort *panned out*. The expression has evolved beyond simply gold mining. Today when circumstances in any area work out successfully, they have *panned out*. So sift through your lists of words, study them well, and things will *pan out* for you on your next vocabulary test.

parlor The French word *parler* means "to speak" or "to talk." That is exactly what happened in a *parlor*, the ancestor of today's living room. The parlor was a room used to receive guests and converse. Later, the hosts and guests would go off to the dining room to take part in the evening's meal. In the past the deceased were laid out in the *parlor*. We still use the term funeral *parlor* today. Parlez-vous in the *parlor*?

patella In ancient Rome a small, shallow pan was called a *patella*. Probably because the kneecap's shape resembles that of the Roman pan, the kneecap was named the *patella* about 400 years ago. *Patina*, the Latin word for dish, is the fine crust or film on bronze or copper objects, especially dishes. Thus, *patella* and patina are related in their origins. Luckily, patina does not grow on one's *patella*!

peace The Latin words *pacem* and *pax* mean "the absence of war" or "*peace*." Native Americans smoked *peace* pipes and "buried the hatchet" to end war. During the 1960s *peace* became a popular word as many Americans, advocating the United States' withdrawal from the fighting in Vietnam, took part in *peace* marches and *peace* demonstrations to stop the war. The *peace* sign, a V formed by the index and middle fingers, was a familiar sign of the times. The efforts of these pacifists, known as *peace*niks, were finally successful. A decade or two later, *peace* or *peace* out meant "goodbye." *Peace*!

peace

"There was never a good war or a bad **peace**."

—Ben Franklin (U.S. statesman)

pedigree Both people and animals may have a *pedigree*. Long ago, genealogists, those who chart a family's tree or list of ancestors, used a three-toed line to show a family's succession.

The French expression *pied de grue* (foot of a crane) was adopted by genealogists to signify the family line because this vertical line that was divided into three branches resembled the foot of a bird called the crane. Since olden English speakers pronounced *pied de grue* as we pronounce *pedigree* today, *pedigree* has come to mean one's list of ancestors. Since you know a *pedigree*'s *pedigree*, you are a crane's foot up on the others.

piggyback

Pigs have nothing to do with a *piggyback*. *Pickpack*, *pickback*, and *pick-a-back* are all older forms of the modern-day *piggyback*. All three of these earlier forms of *piggyback* refer to a picked pack, a pack, or bundle pitched on one's back or shoulders. *Picked pack* or any of the other versions sound much like the word *piggyback*, which still means to carry on the shoulders or back. Now that you know *piggyback*'s history, do you feel that a great weight has been lifted from your back and shoulders?

Piggyback, anyone?

pink slip When a worker receives a *pink slip*, he is fired. Although there seems to be little firm agreement as to how the term came into the language, two suggestions seem possible. Perhaps the discharge paper signaling a worker's dismissal was pink. Thus the term *pink slip*. Then again, the verb *pink* means to stab, something a worker might feel has figuratively happened to him after his company's officials no longer desire his services. Green card, *blue law*, *Purple Heart*, and red carpet are other familiar terms that include colors.

poll How many people favor this presidential candidate? Who is the best athlete of the century? What is the best rock group of the past fifty years? Let's take a *poll*! *Polls*, methods of collecting information, are quite popular today. In England 700 years ago, *pol* was the word for head, and the information seekers who wanted to measure public opinion simply counted heads or *pols*. So use your head in the next *poll*.

poll

"If Rosa Parks had taken a **poll** before she sat down in the bus in Montgomery, she'd still be standing."

—*Mary Frances Berry (U.S. government official and author)*

pooped (*slang*) If you want to know where *pooped* (meaning very tired) began, visit a large sailing vessel. During the 1800s, sailors found that the *poop* or aft (rear) deck of their ships took the most beating during the violent storms. Enormous waves would sometimes severely damage this *poop* deck. The sailors who tended to these problems on the *poop* deck were fatigued. So, if the boat and sailors were lucky enough to make it to port safely, both were *pooped* or exhausted. Are you too *pooped* to watch the waves from the *poop* deck?

posse Derived from the Latin for "power of the county," *posse* was the body of men summoned and required to help the sheriff keep peace or chase lawbreakers in the Old West. People in the 1970s and 1980s called one's group of friends a *posse*. In the more recent hip-hop and rap cultures, the slang word *posse* (or *crew* or *tribe*) referred to the gang that accompanies the gang leader through the streets. Thus, in the world of slang, a *pig* could *bust* a *posse*, *fer sure*!

postman Originally, the Latin word *posita* meant "placed." From that word a *posta* station became a fixed place on a road. Later, the French *poste* was a station for a post (or mail) horse. Riders and their horses were posted at designated intervals along a route to carry mail in a relay setup. The original *postmen* were royal messengers who carried the king's messages by relay to distant locations. Years later, these *postmen* carried actual pieces of mail to the commoners.

Today, political correctness requires that a *postman* or mailman be referred to as a postal worker. With the popularity and quickness of electronic mail (e-mail), the original mail system begun by these hardworking relay *postmen* is now called *snail mail*. How times have changed!

Postal worker

potluck Today, *potluck* refers to having to take whatever is available, with little or no choice. If you select "*potluck*" in a vending machine, you must accept whatever item the machine drops down. You have no choice! How did potluck come to mean little or no choice? Some 400 years ago, lower class people often threw their leftovers into a simmering iron *pot* on an open fire. Unexpected visitors were usually invited to sit down to eat with the family. Whatever foods were in the *pot* that day, maybe something delicious, maybe something awful, made up the meal. It was all a matter of *luck*! So the original "*pot luck* people" were both hungry and willing to take a risk.

pretzel This tasty, salty snack has both Latin and German roots. The Latin root means "a type of biscuit baked in the shape of folded arms." The German root designates "having branches (or arms)." A *pretzel*, with a little imagination on your part, fits both definitions. When *pretzels* are placed in front of people, everyone digs right in. Nobody's arms are folded.

Pretzel made in the shape of folded arms

Procrustean Here is a rather long word with a rather interesting history. Procrustes was a Greek mythological giant who loved to seize travelers, tie them to either a long or a short bed, and torture them. How did he torture them? He would either cut or stretch them! If the traveler was longer than the bed, the victim's body was cut to fit perfectly onto the bed. If the traveler was too short, Procrustes would stretch the victim's limbs out with weights until the victim's body fit the bed precisely. Today *Procrustean* means any ruthless, drastic, or arbitrary action designed to secure conformity at any cost. Such merciless disregard for

individual differences goes back to the idea of the mean Procrustes. Remember that the history of the word *Procrustean* cannot be stretched out or shortened to fit someone's arbitrary wishes.

prodigy

Five hundred years ago, the Roman word *prodige* meant "an extraordinary sign or omen." Over time *prodige* became the English word *prodigy*, but its meaning stayed the same. By the early 1600s, *prodigy* meant any marvel or wonder. Almost 100 years later, it referred to any person or animal with exceptional qualities. Finally, today *prodigy* usually refers to a child of unusual talent in a specific area (or areas). A fourteen-year-old college graduate is definitely a *prodigy*.

profane

Often words with the prefix "*pro-*" have positive meanings. *Profit*, *proper*, and *prolific* are some examples. *Profane*, taken from the Latin combination of "*pro*" (before) and "*fanum*" (temple), has primarily negative meanings. Many years ago, those who were considered unholy were not allowed within the temple's walls. They were "outside the temple" or *profane*. Today, one who is *profane* or one who uses profanity shows disrespect or irreverence for sacred things.

profane

"No facts are to me sacred; none are **profane**; I simply experiment, an endless seeker, with no past at my back."

—Ralph Waldo Emerson (U.S. philosopher, poet, and essayist)

punk

(*slang*) This unfortunate word has never been associated with anything positive! Scientists gave the name *punk* to the "decayed, rotten wood used as kindling." Since the early 1900s, *punk out* has meant "to cowardly back out from a fight." *Hoodlums*, those troublemakers of the 1950s, were called *punks*. Even *punk rock*, the name given to the musical style of the 1970s, was often associated with rude, offensive performers. Hip-hoppers called weak people *punks*. Lastly, in the 1990s, jerks were called *punks*. Maybe you can be the one to give *punk* a good name. Now don't *punk out* from doing so.

Purple Heart

This U.S. military award is given to members of the armed forces who are wounded or killed in military conflict. George Washington initiated this important medal during the Revolutionary War. The award was established in 1782. Washington wanted the *Purple Heart* recipient to "wear over the left breast the figure of a heart in purple cloth, or silk, edged with narrow lace or binding." Roll out the red carpet for those who have been awarded the *Purple Heart.*

The Purple Heart is on this man's hat.

pussyfoot

A person who *pussyfoots* either moves with great caution or stealth (like a cat) or shies away from taking a firm stand on an issue. The origin of the word is debatable. Some say it comes from the catlike actions of Marshall William Eugene Johnson of the Oklahoma Indian Territory. Johnson, a famed advocate of the Prohibition movement, earned the nickname *Pussyfoot* because of his uncanny ability to sneak up on lawbreakers. He convicted 4,400 people from 1908 to 1911! Others say that President Theodore Roosevelt either *coined* or popularized this informal word in its other sense. Because *pussyfoot's* origin is not agreed upon by all word historians, some may *pussyfoot* around *pussyfoot's* history.

putt-putt

In golf, a *putt* is the shot that is made on the *putting* green in an attempt to roll the ball into the hole. Many miniature golf courses are known as *putt-putt* courses. Why? Since each shot is much like a *putt,* the golfer simply *putts* and then *putts* again. Since the course is very small, there are no drives. Just *putt, putt,* and *putt* some more! *Putt-putt* is also the chugging or popping sounds made by the engine of a car, boat, or another vehicle. Legend has it that a car salesman, trying to sell a car to a prospective buyer and wanting to hide the noises made by an older engine, would pack the car's joints and pistons with a sticky substance. Often this gummy material was putty. This led clever cartoonists to use "*putt-putt*" (from putty) as the comic strip sound of an aging motor. Do people drive their *putt-putts* when they go to play *putt-putt*?

python This name for the world's second largest snake (the anaconda is the largest) is derived from the Greek word meaning "to rot." Legend has it that the first *python*, a mythological serpent who was found in the caves near Greece's Mount Parnassus, was killed by Apollo and subsequently dried up and rotted in the sun's heat. Today, a *python* is a very large, nonpoisonous snake that squeezes its enemy to death. Now that's an awful way to die—and rot away.

A python snake looks for prey.

quarantine

When you think of *quarantine*, immediately think of forty! Through the years *quarantine* has meant many things—all associated with forty. In the early 1500s, *quarantine* was the name of the number of days a widow could legally remain in her dead husband's house (much before women's liberation became popular!). One hundred years later, *quarantine* meant the period of days that a ship suspected of carrying disease had to be isolated. In addition, a *quarantine* was the number of days that travelers coming from a plague-ridden country had to stay away from others in the new country. Nowadays, a *quarantine*, which is thankfully not as frequent an event as in the past, is the period of isolation (no specific number of days) that is usually associated with disease. Even a patient in the hospital can be in isolation until he or she recovers. So stay healthy and avoid a *quarantine*.

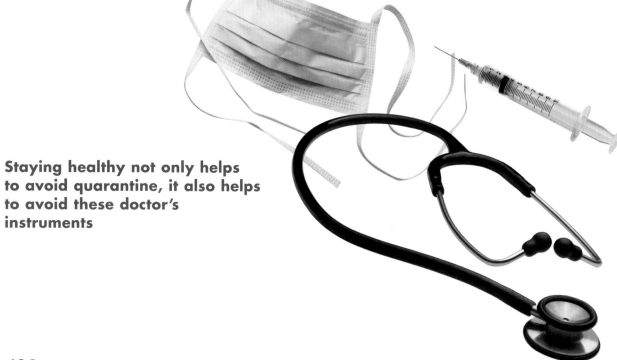

Staying healthy not only helps to avoid quarantine, it also helps to avoid these doctor's instruments

rabbi The Hebrew word *rabbi* means "my master" or "my lord." For the past 600 years, *rabbi* has been the name for a Jewish religious leader who is both a scholar and a teacher of Jewish law. Today a *rabbi* is an ordained Jew who is the spiritual head of a synagogue, a word of Greek origin that means "a gathering together." The words *abba* and *abbot* are closely related in meaning to *rabbi*.

A rabbi reads from a scroll.

radar During World War II, Robert Alexander Watson Watt developed the radiolocator. This device, first employed by the British forces, used high-frequency radio waves to locate the enemy. Have you ever heard of the radiolocator? In 1943, the U.S. Navy renamed the device and called it "*ra*dio *d*etecting *a*nd *r*anging," better known as *radar*. Currently, the speeds of cars and baseball pitches are measured with *radar* guns. What other uses would Mr. Watt find for *radar* today?

109

rap (*slang*) Here is a word that has had (and continues to have) a very interesting life! Several centuries ago, a *rap* was a severe blow, as in a *rap* on the head. Later, a formal complaint or the act of testifying against someone also became known as a *rap*. About 200 years ago, a *rap* was also a prison sentence. So a criminal headed for jail could have a *rap* sheet—a list of crimes he committed. The hippies like to *rap* (discuss or talk) about almost anything. They held discussions called *rap* sessions. People probably *rapped* at New York's 1969 Woodstock Festival attended by more than 400,000. Today, *rap*, a combination of *rap* (to talk) and *rap* (as in rapid), is a popular musical style. *Rappers* are into *rap* music, a fast-paced style of music that uses much rhythm and rhyme. This style of music, started in the late 1970s, is part of a cultural movement. Want to *rap* about *rap*?

red-letter day Since the 1400s, holidays, festivals, and saints' days have been marked in red ink on calendars. These *red-letter days* were memorable or joyous days or events. Christmas Day and Easter Sunday were marked in red ink. More recently, a *red-letter day* has come to mean any memorable or lucky day. Is tomorrow going to be your *red-letter day*, Lucky?

red tape Ever hear people complain about how they had to go through so much *red tape* in order to do something? Over 200 years ago in England, lawyers and government officials used red-colored tape or ribbon to tie up their legal documents. Many of these documents were probably both tedious and time-consuming to read. Today, excessive and time-consuming rules and procedures, especially in dealing with official forms and actions, are known as *red tape*. How much *red tape* will you need to go through to tape and sell a Cincinnati Reds tape?

rehash Storytellers will *rehash* stories that people have enjoyed. Sometimes people will *rehash* old arguments. *Rehash*, "to bring up or go over again," comes from the French for hatchet, the cutting tool. Hash (not to be confused with hashish!) was the small cut-up pieces of meat left over from the original larger cut of meat. Rather than throw these smaller pieces of meat away, cooks warmed them up and served them the next day. Although these leftovers were from the same cut of meat, it was, so to speak, in a new form. The meat had been *rehashed*! Why do adults like to *rehash* stories about how difficult things were when they were kids? Now that is a meaty issue.

robot Czechoslovakian Karel Capek's 1921 play, *R. U. R.* (*Rossum's Universal Robots*), featured mechanical men called *robots*. The playwright *coined* the word *robot* from the Czech word for work (*robata*) and the earlier word *rabu* for slave. These *robots*, built by Rossum's Universal, were slaves that did manual work for human beings. In operating rooms today, *robots* perform some mediacal operations on human beings. What will *robots* be doing 100 years from now?

Robots are designed to help human beings.

rock and roll In the early 1950s, Alan Freed, a disc jockey in Cleveland, Ohio, called the type of music that teens danced to *"rock and roll."* This type of music evolved from music called "rhythm and blues." *Rock and roll* featured electric guitars, lyrics primarily for teens, and performers such as Elvis Presley. This style of music quickly became the favorite sound of the baby boomers. Today's rock music is a descendant of *rock and roll*. How much *rocking and rolling* can the baby boomers do today?

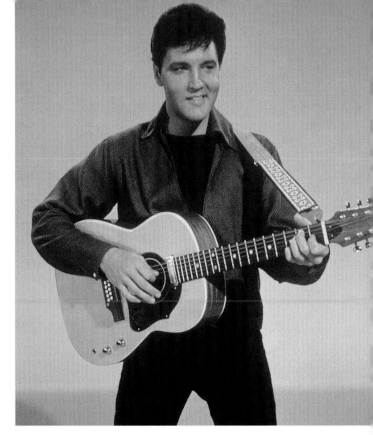

Elvis Presley

Roger Walkie-talkie users and others who use other types of radio communicators are familiar with the word *roger*. *Roger*, originally used by airplane pilots using radio communications, indicated to the person on the other end of the radio message that "your message is received and understood." *Roger*, meaning *"received,"* was the code word for the letter R. Other words used in radio terminology include affirm (yes), negative (no), advise (let me know what you want), and wilco (I will comply). *Roger?*

roster Long ago in Holland, an army man's duties were usually written down on ruled paper that resembled a gridiron (a framework of metal bars or wires on which to broil meat or fish). Noting the paper's arrangement of lines, the Dutch called this sheet a *rooster*, from the Dutch word, *roosten*, meaning "to roast." So, the Dutch *rooster* of yesteryear is today's English-language *roster*. Football players whose names appear on a *roster* compete on a gridiron.

round robin Some sports tournaments are set up in a *round robin* format. In this arrangement, each team (or entrant) is matched against another. Thus, no one can complain that the tournament was unfair since everybody plays each other at least once.

In this way, no one receives preferential treatment. The idea of a *round robin* began in France in the 1600s. There government officials signed their grievance petitions on a *ruban rond* (round ribbon) that was attached (in circular form) to the documents. In this way, no one official could be accused of signing the document first (starting the grievance) and perhaps getting himself into serious trouble as the group's *scapegoat*. Each signer was given the special treatment. Later, for the same reasons, the British navy used the *round robin* plan to air their complaints. Our softball team, the Robins, won the summer *round robin* tournament for the third consecutive year.

rubberneck Next time you are stuck in traffic, you might be a victim of the *rubberneck*. Since the early 1900s, *rubberneck* has described the person who is offensively curious and needs to know everything that is going on about him. Thus, the overly nosy motorist who feels the need to see the effects of the motor vehicle accident, even if it is several highway lanes away, is a *rubberneck*. His neck is apparently "made of rubber" and allows him to easily turn to see what is happening around him.

rugby This form of football, featuring 15-player teams and continuous action, is popular in Europe. Many Americans also enjoy the game,

Rugby match

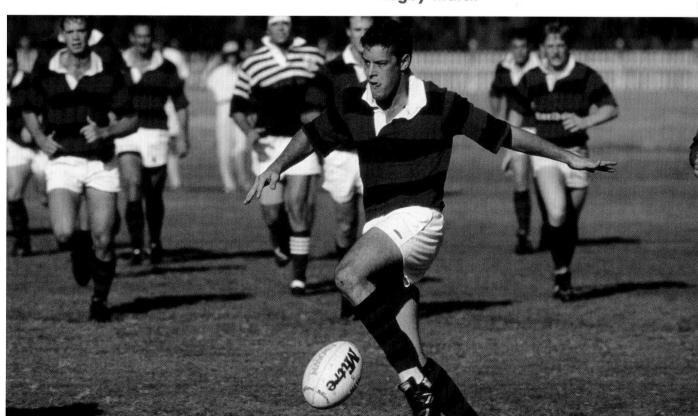

especially college students. Even though it can sometimes be a pretty rough game, there are both men's and women's teams on the college level. The sport was given its name because it started at the *Rugby* School in Warwickshire, England, in 1823. Apparently, during a soccer game at this famous boys' school, a student picked up the ball and ran with it. The rest is, as they say, history. Thanks to that *Rugby* boy, those who play *rugby* have been having a ball ever since.

rummage People enjoy going to *rummage* sales to make purchases. The shopper who *rummages* through the items at *rummage* sales searches through (*rummages*) the items. *Rummage* comes from a French word, *arrumage*, meaning the act of arranging a ship's cargo. When the cargo was damaged during the ship's voyage, these damaged goods were put up for sale at warehouses. These *arrumage* sales evolved into our *rummage* sales that also featured low-quality goods for purchase. Today, a *rummage* sale is full of both old and new articles whose sales will usually go to charities.

Rx Next time you are in a drugstore, look for the symbol *Rx*, pronounced "RX." The R in the symbol is from the Latin word for "take this," and the slant across the R's leg is the sign of Jupiter, the Roman god of medicine. *Rx* is designated as the remedy suggested for a medical problem. Look for this symbol on a medicine bottle or anywhere in the store. *Take this* advice and make Jupiter proud.

As you can see by the Rx printed on it, this pad is for prescriptions.

salt Because *salt* was so greatly prized during ancient times, part of a Roman soldier's pay (or salary) was given in *salt*. A good Roman soldier was supposedly "worth his *salt*." Through the years, *salt* has enjoyed other positive associations. In the olden days, if you sat "above the *salt*," you sat in an honored position at the dining table. A fine, noble person was the "*salt* of the earth." Would you accept *salt* as part of your salary?

Salt was a form of payment in Roman times.

sandwich John Montagu, the fourth earl of *Sandwich*, lived during the 1700s. He often gambled for twenty-four hours straight! During one of these marathon gambling sessions, he became so involved in gambling that he did not even stop to eat. Instead, he ordered his servant to bring him two thick slices of roast beef between two pieces of toasted bread. In this way Montagu kept the cards clean and kept the game going. He also gave his name, *sandwich*, to this bread and meat combination. And that's no bologna!

Sandwich

Saturday Saturn, the Roman god of time, seed, and sowing, is remembered on *Saturday*, or "Saturn's day." In Greek mythology, Cronus is identified with the Roman Saturn. Thus, Cronus, associated with time, is also somewhat responsible for the words *chronic, chronological, chronology,* and *chronometer*—all time words! Could Saturn place the days of the week in chronological order—ending with *Saturday*?

scapegoat A passage from the Bible talks of two goats: one goat for the Lord and another for a *scapegoat*. The goat that was randomly chosen to be the Lord's was sacrificed as the "sin offering." In this way, the people's sins were placed on the head of the other goat, which was subsequently released into the wilderness. Essentially, this second goat both escaped death and bore the blame for the others' sins. Today, the person who "bears the blame for the mistakes or sins of others" is called a *scapegoat*. The competitor who is blamed for the team's loss is called a goat, short for *scapegoat*. Fortunately, that goat (or *scapegoat*) is not forced into the wilderness.

Scrooge Ebenezer *Scrooge*, the ill-tempered miser who later becomes a charitable humanitarian, is a character in the 1843 short story, "A Christmas Carol," by British writer Charles Dickens. Visited by the three ghosts, *Scrooge* changes his evil ways and helps those around him, especially Bob Cratchit and his sickly son, Tiny Tim. Unfortunately, *Scrooge* is not remembered for his newfound generosity. Instead, today a *Scrooge* is a hard, miserly person who dislikes people.

scuba You can only hold your breath underwater for so long. If you use the *s*elf-contained *u*nderwater *b*reathing *a*pparatus (*scuba*), you could stay under for much longer. Will someone ever invent a better underwater breathing apparatus than the *scuba*? Don't hold your breath!

Scuba diver

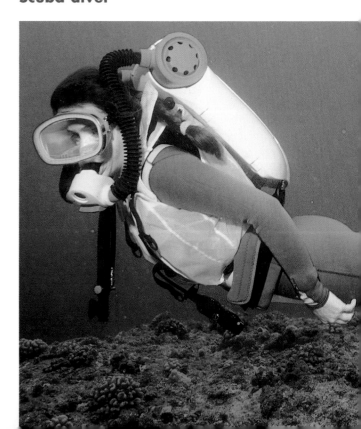

116

September

Septem is the Latin word for seven. In ancient times when *March* began the calendar year, *September* was the seventh month, so its name is appropriate. When the calendar was changed more than 2,000 years ago, *September* was moved from the seventh to the ninth month but the name remained the same. Thirty days hath (the ninth month) *September*...

seventh-inning stretch

Ever wonder why fans at the ballpark stand to *stretch* before the home team comes to bat in the *seventh inning*? This tradition has been part of baseball for more than 100 years. Some say that it began when President Howard Taft stood up to *stretch* in

These fans can't wait for the seventh inning stretch of this baseball game.

the seventh inning at a Washington Senators game. The crowd, out of respect for President Taft, also stood up and *stretched*. Others believe that the tradition started with Brother Jasper, the baseball coach and head of discipline at Manhattan College. Supposedly, Jasper told the Manhattan College students to stand and *stretch* before their team, the home team, came to bat in the *seventh inning*. Believe what you will since neither story is a *stretch*.

shampoo Hundreds of years ago, servants in India massaged the bodies of their masters after hot baths. The words *champo* and *shampoo*, meaning "to press," were used to define this pressing and massaging with oils. In time, many travelers visiting India came to enjoy this *shampoo* by Indian servants. When the *shampoo* ritual reached England, it was not met with the same enthusiasm since only the rich could afford the luxury of a servant who could *shampoo* the body. By 1860, *shampoo* came to describe the simple washing and rubbing of the hair. So whether you are a rich person or a servant, your scalp and hair need frequent *shampoos*.

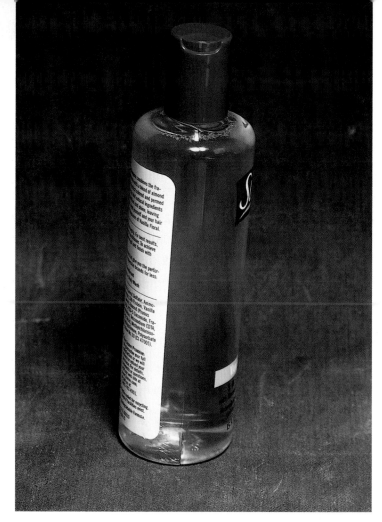

Bottle of shampoo

shock jock A new type of radio personality was introduced to American listeners in the 1980s. The *shock jock* was the controversial talk-radio disc jockey who was usually quite offensive and shocking in both his language and his program's content. This offensive and often abusive radio performer could be entertaining to some listeners and obnoxious to others. Either way, this *shock jock* was shocking!

shoddy Today you would not want to be seen in a *shoddy* (inferior in quality) outfit. But the Civil War soldiers (1860s) had to settle for uniforms made of cheap, woolen material that the textile workers called *shoddy*. Needless to say, these uniforms did not last long since they were made of second—(or even third-) rate material. Hopefully, this explanation is not too *shoddy*.

sideburns

Ambrose Burnside, a Union general during the Civil War, sported a mustache and interesting sidebar whiskers (hair grown in front of the ears). This style of hair was so distinctive that his name became attached to these whiskers. But there was a catch! The two syllables of his last name were reversed, and *sideburn* (not Burnside) became the name of these whiskers. Elvis Presley, the 1950s-1970s rock and roll legend, wore *sideburns*. Before long, many men were growing *sideburns* to look like Elvis. Too bad that even with (or without) *sideburns*, they could not perform as well as Elvis.

General Ambrose Burnside with his sideburns

siren

It is hard to believe that sailors could be attracted to the *Sirens*, creatures that were half-woman—and half-bird! In ancient Greek mythology, these *Sirens*, daughters of the Greek sea god, lured men to their deaths with their singing. Broken boards from the ships and the blood and bones of these dead sailors who tried to swim to the Sirens' island attested to the powers of the *Sirens*. On one particular voyage, Ulysses, tied to the ship's mast, passed the *Sirens'* island, heard the Sirens' singing, and lived to tell about it. Today, a *siren*, like those on fire trucks and ambulances, is used to warn people, not to seduce and kill them.

A police car siren

Civil rights era lunch counter sit-in

sit-in The American Civil Rights Movement of the early 1960s popularized the *sit-in*. This nonviolent type of protest was used by protesting African Americans who took the seats reserved "for white people only" at the lunch counters of restaurants primarily in the South. They would "*sit-in*" until they were either jailed or served. Besides these racial type of *sit-ins*, protesters against the Vietnam War and other important issues staged *sit-ins*. College campuses were often the scene of such protests. Will the *sit-in* ever regain its popularity among protesters?

slave During the Middle Ages (476-1450), the Slavic people of Central Europe—primarily the Russians and Czechs—were conquered by the Germanic peoples and then sold into *slavery*. *Sclavus* was the name associated with these subjected Slavs. Over time, *Sclavus* became our modern day word *slave*. So, for better or for worse, *slave* trade, *slave* drivers, and *slave* holders owe their existence to the Slavs!

slave

"Slaves were expected to sing as well as to work. A silent **slave** was not liked, either by masters or overseers."

—*Frederick Douglass (U.S. lecturer and author)*

slipshod In the late1500s, men commonly wore *slipshoes* (loose slippers). These shoes had originally been created for indoor use only. Careless men were often too lazy to change into different shoes before going outdoors. The more respectable citizens looked down on these careless individuals who, it is rumored, were bold enough to wear these *slipshoes* to religious services. In time, *slipshoes* became *slipshod*, a word meaning sloppy. Presently, *slipshod* means careless, as in one's appearance or quality of work.

smog For the past 100 years, smog, a blend of *sm*oke and f*og*, has been used to describe the harmful air quality created by pollution. Toxic gases and fine particles combine to create poor air quality. Often, *smog* hangs over an industrial city, creating health and other kinds of problems. Recycling and *carpooling* are some ways people have tried to reduce *smog*. How have you tried to reduce *smog*?

Smog over Houston, Texas, a city that has recently become the smog capital of the country

snail mail When asked to name a very slow-moving creature, you might think of the snail. Although the national postal systems of the world might not want to hear this, their traditional present-day system of delivering mail is sarcastically called *snail mail*. Why? When contrasted to the speed of modern information carriers such as e-mails and *faxes*, the current mail service is quite slow. Thus for some people, *snail mail* is an appropriate name. Even though today's postal system might be slow, think of how slow the older postal delivery methods—mail coach, mail stage, mail boat, mail train, and mail truck—must have been. Now there are some snails!

sniper More than five centuries ago, the bird called the *snipe* was often spotted near marshes and swamps. The snipe's flesh was prized. This clever bird was too fast and aware of the hunters using bows and arrows. More often than not, these hunters could not get near enough to get a good shot at the elusive snipe. When improved firearms were introduced in the 1500s, the hunters were then able to hide in the woods near the marshes and wait for the birds to appear. Once they did, these snipes became easy prey. The powerfully armed *snipers*, concealed in the growth, proved too much for the seemingly defenseless snipes. Today, a *sniper* is one who shoots at an enemy from any hidden position—not just in marshes and swamps.

soap opera Starting on radio and then moving over to television, the *soap opera* has been part of the American media since the late 1930s. Today's *soap opera*, usually a thirty- or sixty-minute program, presents domestic situations in a melodramatic or sentimental fashion. Because many of the original sponsors of this type of program were *soap* manufacturers, the word *soap* seemed appropriate. Perhaps the word *opera* is taken from the horse opera, a type of entertainment popular in the 1920s. The western, a show set in the western United States during the frontier expansion, is the more modern version of the horse opera. Remember to use soap to wash away the tears after watching a *soap opera*.

soul music Combining rhythm and blues and gospel music, the black singers of the 1960s brought *soul music* to the top of the musical charts. The great emotional and spiritual quality of the culture manifested itself in this *soul music*. Other terms with the word *soul* include *soul* brothers, *soul* sisters, and *soul* food (e.g.,collard greens and black-eyed peas).

Soul singer Stevie Wonder

southpaw If you are a left-handed person, you may have been called a *southpaw*. For more than 100 years, *lefties* have been called *southpaws*. It all started with Finley Peter Dunne, a sportswriter who was covering a baseball game in Chicago. Dunne reported that since home plate was to the west in this baseball park, the pitcher threw the baseball with the hand (or paw) that was on his south side. In time, the slang word *southpaw* described any left-handed person. Hopefully, this explanation did not throw you, Lefty!

spazz (*slang*) This word for an uncoordinated person had its beginnings in the word *spastic*—one who suffers from spastic (involuntary muscular contractions) paralysis.

Although the more formal spastic is a serious word associated with a medical condition, the slang *spazz* is generally used in a teasing or mildly mocking sense. "What a *spazz*!" might be said of the person who has just tripped over his own shoelaces. She who has thrown a tantrum might hear another exclaim, "Don't *spazz* out on us!" And that's the jazz on *spazz*.

spoonerism When someone intends to say, "a well-oiled bicycle," and instead says, "a well-boiled icicle," he has furnished you with an example of a *spoonerism*. Named after nineteenth-century minister and history professor, Reverend William Archibald Spooner, a *spoonerism* is the unintentional interchange of sounds, usually the initial sounds, in two or more words. Spooner's slip of the tongue assuredly made for some funny moments. His intended "a crushing blow" became "a blushing crow." His "battle ships and cruisers" became "cattle ships and bruisers," and "Our Lord is a loving shepherd" became "Our Lord is a shoving leopard." Whether these humorous mistakes were due to Spooner's nervousness or to his thinking too quickly (or slowly), he has left behind some memorable lines.

static (*slang*) Those electrical discharges that interfere with radio or television reception are known as *static*. They cause trouble (and annoyance) for others! Our hip-hop *static* means exactly that—trouble. To the hippies, *static* was a form of criticism, as in "I don't need *static* from you. Leave me alone!" *Static* has also meant quarreling and, before that, "conversation that meant nothing," much like that which *static* brings to your radio or television reception— nothing but trouble! Now don't give any *static* about *static*'s definition. So even if you think you are the *big cheese*, please don't give us any trouble because we will give little reception to your *static*.

stewardess Originally, a *steward* was a "sty ward" or the "keeper of the pigs." In time the *steward* became the man in charge of the affairs of an estate or a large household. Later the *steward* was one who was in charge of the estate's food and drink. The sea *steward* was an attendant who looked after the passengers' comforts and an officer who managed the ship's stores and was responsible for the food and drink on the ship. Lastly, the female flight attendant was called a *steward* or *stewardess*, the "-ess" signifying the feminine gender. Today both the airline's *steward* and *stewardess* are called flight attendants.

Stewardesses make air travel more comfortable.

stoic Some people cannot hide their emotions during life's good times or bad times. Others remain *stoic* or *stoical* because they can hold back their feelings and choose to practice patience instead. In ancient Greece, the philosopher Zeno and his pupils were called *stoics* because they met in the *stoas* (shops) of Athens, a city known for its education. Zeno taught his students to accept life's turns calmly. "What will be will be" was his advice.

stoked (*slang*) When you are very happy, excited, or really enthusiastic about something, you are *stoked*. This slang word probably had its origins in the 1960s from the verb *stoke*, which means "to stir up and feed fuel to the fire." So when the fire is really heated up, it has been *stoked* well. And when a person is really heated up or excited about something, he or she is *stoked*! Are you *stoked* about learning the history of so many words? Hope so!

stump The expression "to *stump*" means to remove a *stump* (the lower end of a tree remaining in the ground after most of it has been removed). Its informal meaning is "to puzzle or baffle." The two definitions are linked to the same story. Those who built log cabins and other houses in wooded areas needed to remove the trees on the land in order to have enough room to build the home. Cutting the trees down was usually the easy part; removing the *stumps* was the hard job! It took a certain talent to remove the *stump* the correct way. At times, even the most skilled woodsman was not able to remove a particular *stump*. He was "*stumped*" or "puzzled." Have you ever been *stumped* by a test question?

sudden death
Fortunately, everyone involved in a sporting event's *sudden death* lives to tell about it! Coined in the early 1970s, the term *sudden death* defines a short, extra period of time played if the score is tied at the end of the regular game. The team that scores first wins in this *sudden death* period. The losing team, so to speak, dies suddenly. Today, both football games and golfing matches have a *sudden death* rule. Remember that all players live to tell about it.

Sunday The ancient people named the first day of the week in honor of the sun. *Sunday* has traditionally been regarded as a day of worship and rest. In late 1700 colonial New England, *blue laws*, which prohibited certain activities, were enacted to ensure that *Sunday* would be a holy and restful day. The French, keeping the religious importance to the weekend days, named Saturday, *samedi*, a word associated with the Sabbath (day of worship). They named *Sunday dimanche* (from a Latin phrase meaning the Lord's day). Are *Sundays* any sunnier that the other six days of the week?

super (*slang*) In the mid-1800s, *super* meant first-rate or excellent! In today's youth slang, *super* still means the same. *Super*! This word of superior quality can also function as a prefix whose meaning varies from "over" and "above," as in *super*structure, to "greater" or "better," as in *super*market and *super*woman, to "extra," as in *super*fluous and *super*tax. Can you think of five more words that begin with *super*? You can? *Super*!

supercalifragilisticexpialidocious P. L. Travers wrote *Mary Poppins*, a children's book published in 1934. It later became a popular 1964 Disney movie. The 34-letter word *supercalifragilisticexpialidocious* is taken from a nonsense song featured in this film. What does this long word mean? *Supercalifragilisticexpialidocious* is defined as the greatest, the very best of all! If you can spell this word, you have earned the right to be called *supercalifragilisticexpialidocious*!

surf Some think that *surf*, or an alternate form of the word, originally came from India and meant a rushing sound. By 1917, *surf* came to mean to ride on a *surf*board atop the crest of a wave. "*Surf's up*" was a popular exclamation since the waves were good enough to ride. So was "hang ten" (to *surf* with ten toes over the front of the surfboard). *Surfing* also had a different meaning. From the 1950s on, television watchers who switched from channel to channel, often using a remote (a wireless remote control), were said to be *surfing*. By the 1990s, *surf* also came to mean to move from site to site on the Internet. Will there be a day when one will be able to *surf* the Net while *surfing* the waves? Wait and see...

This dude is surfing in the ocean.

Little girl in a big sweater

sweater

A woolen vest or jersey has been called a *sweater* for over 100 years. Yet, for almost 200 years, clothing garments worn to help a person sweat and lose weight have been called *sweaters*. Another meaning of *sweater* came into the language in the late 1880s. This *sweater* was a person who "sweated" others. The sweater would hire tailors and needle-women to work long hours for low wages in terrible working conditions such as a poorly lit or a poorly ventilated factory. This workplace was commonly called a sweatshop. Children were even hired to work in these sweatshops!

In time, reforms, such as doing away with child labor and establishing a minimum wage and healthier working conditions, helped to put an end to sweatshops. Sweatshops are illegal in the United States. Today American people who detest such inhumane working conditions loudly protest the existence of any sweatshop—even if it is not in the United States.

sweet (*slang*) Walter Payton, the late, great Chicago Bears running back, was called "*Sweet*ness" by both sportscasters and football fans. Why? He was something great, something really *sweet*! His swiftness and agility as a football carrier made it very difficult to tackle him. Decades before Payton was born, *sweet* meant "something good," as in a *sweet* vacation or a *sweet* job. Then jazzmen also used *sweet* to designate straight music that was "played as written." Such music must have also been *sweet* to the ear! Today, *sweet* is a term of admiration, as was the case with Hall of Famer Walter Payton. He was *sweet* on his feet.

sweet

"Success is **sweet** and sweeter if long delayed and gotten through many struggles and defeats."

—Amos Bronson Alcott (U.S. teacher, philosopher, and reformer)

talking head This expression came into wide use in the late 1960s. A television image of a person (usually a newsperson or a talk show host or guest) talking on the screen often showed only the talker's head and a bit of the upper body. To many viewers, the image looked like a *talking head*. Who are some of the *talking heads* you see on television these days?

tag banger (*slang*) *Tag*, as a label, started almost 200 years ago. A *dog tag* is the canine's identification tag or license. It is also the slang term for the military identification soldiers wear about their necks. In the 1980s, a *tag* was the nickname or identification mark that was either written or sprayed by a graffiti artist. Often these *tags* were found on subway cars, sides of buildings, and bridges. A *tag banger* is the *graffiti* artist who leaves only his signature. *Taki 183* was a *popular tag* banger whose name appeared in many places.

Elizabeth Dole is one of many talking heads seen on television today.

tantalize

Today, *tantalize* means to tease or promise something that is held back or not given. *Tantalize* owes its existence to *Tantalus*, an ancient Greek king. *Tantalus* told the secrets of the gods to humans, and he was punished by being placed in a pool up to his chin in Hades, the Greek underworld. Here he was teased and tortured, a *tantalizing* experience, for sure! How? When he reached above him for a piece of tasty fruit from the tree branch, the fruit would be pulled just out of his reach. And when Tantalus bent down to drink the water, the water level would drop—just far enough that it was barely out of his reach. Unlike the misbehaving *Tantalus*, you can now reach, grab, and enjoy this *tantalizing* story.

tar and feather

If you were a British seaman who was caught stealing in the 1100s, you were *tarred and feathered*. Your body was smeared with tar, *and* feathers were placed over the tar. Ugh! During the American Revolution, British loyalists were *tarred and feathered* by the rebels. The 1791 Bill of Rights ended this inhumane punishment. Today, *tarred and feathered* means simply to be publicly embarrassed— still a sticky issue.

tarantula

This large, hairy spider with a poisonous bite was found in abundance many years ago in the city of Taranto, a city in southern Italy, and so this arachnid is aptly named *tarantula*. More than 600 years ago, a bizarre disease, accompanied

Tarantulas are big, hairy spiders.

by severe jerking of a person's limbs, found its way through parts of Europe. This sickness supposedly caused people to dance, probably because the limbs were moving pretty well already! People in Italy superstitiously thought that the disease was caused by the *tarantula*'s bite. Thus, the abnormality was named *tarantism*. (Today this disorder of the nervous system is called *chorea*, from the Greek word for *dance*.) As this epidemic made its way throughout Europe, a dance thought to help its victims overcome the disease became popular—especially in southern Italy. This dance was given the name tarantella, a popular dance at weddings today.

taxicab In 1907 Harry N. Allen, angered by the high cost of horse-drawn carriages in New York City, introduced the taximeter cab. Though he would not have been aware of it (Allen was more interested in the cost of getting around the city), the name he selected for the new mode of transportation was interesting and would last. It is a combination of the Greek *taxa* (charge or cost), the Greek *meter* (measure), and the French *cabriolet* (cab). Later the name was shortened to *taxicab* and finally to today's *taxi*. The *taxi* driver is also called a hack. Could you hack being driven around New York City in a hack's cab? Henry N. Allen could!

Taxi cab

Teddy bear

teddy bear The toy we call a teddy bear is a stuffed figure named after Theodore (Teddy) Roosevelt, the twenty-sixth president of the United States (1901-1909), an avid hunter. Roosevelt's hunting expeditions occasioned a humorous poem and cartoons printed in *The New York Times* of January 7, 1906. Before long, stuffed toy bears (commemorating Teddy's hunts) were imported from Germany and became instantly popular in America. How well did Teddy bear that? Hunt for an answer!

teenybopper (*slang*) In the mid-1960s, the word *teenybopper* became part of the English language. A *teenybopper* was a pre-teen or young teenager, most often a female, who strongly identified with the hippie culture and the pop music culture. These *teenyboppers* influenced the fashion world with their trendy and sometimes outrageous clothes. *Teenybopper* probably came from the words teenager and small (*teeny*) and *bop* (to walk in an easy but strutting way). Fortunately, or unfortunately, *teenybopper* is no longer as fashionable a word today.

Teenybopper, 1955. Not much has changed in the past 50 years

ten-foot pole Nearly 200 years ago, a *ten-foot pole* was used as a land surveying instrument. Though with time the instrument was used less frequently, the term *ten-foot pole*, meaning a certain distance, gained popularity. How frequently is the term used today? Do not touch that question with a *ten-foot pole*!

third degree When people feel that they are asked too many questions, they will often ask, "What is this? The *third degree*?" This expression began with the Masons (men whose work involves building with

stone, brick, and concrete) in the late 1800s. The *Third Degree*, the highest achievement among the Masons, was not earned without much hard work—and numerous questions. The person who achieved the *Third Degree* had to sit through many long examinations and answer many difficult and challenging questions. It was a grueling experience! We promise that you will not be given the *third degree* about the Masons' *third degree* story.

thug Almost 800 years ago in India, a group of religious fanatics murdered people (often by strangling), purportedly as a religious duty. After strangling the victim, the *assassin* would rob, or *thag* (Sanskrit for *cheat*), the person. For more than 600 years, these *thags*, who often became wealthy through their gruesome actions, ravaged India. During the 1800s, when India became part of the British Empire, the English pronounced *thag* as *thug*. The British took care of many captured *thugs*, often by hanging these criminals. Today, a *thug* is a rough *hoodlum*, robber, or gangster.

Thursday Thor was the Norse (Norwegian) god of thunder, war, and strength. He made thunder when he drove his chariot pulled by goats across the sky. Thor, the son of Woden (*Wednesday*) and Freya (*Friday*), was easily the bravest and most powerful of the Norse gods. He, too, was given his own day of the week. Thus, *Thursday* is Thor's day. The French dedicated their word for *Thursday*, jeudi, to Jupiter (Jove), the Roman god of thunder and the skies. Say this five time fast, "*Thursday* is named for Thor the Thunderer."

tom-tom When the British were in the East Indies, they heard the word *tam-tam*, a word from the Hindi language of India that imitated the sound made by hitting the drum. The British changed *tam-tam* to *tom-tom* and gave this name to the drum used by the American Indians. Did you get a bang out of this *tom-tom* story?

top dollar When a customer pays the full-value price for an item, he or she pays *top dollar*. In a game of poker, the chip on top of the bidding pile is higher and worth more than the other chips in the pile. It is literally the *top dollar*. Do you prefer bargain hunting or paying *top dollar*?

tragedy It is hard to believe that our modern *tragedy*, a story having an unhappy or even disastrous ending, was once associated with goats. *Tragoidia*, *tragedy*'s Greek ancestor, literally means "goat song." Since this word is so old, a few educated guesses as to why goat and *tragedy* are forever linked together are in order. Maybe *tragedy* is an appropriate word because a goat was awarded to the best actor in the ancient Greek plays. Perhaps *tragedy* is befitting because some actors (there were no actresses allowed on the Greek stage) or singers in these Greek *tragedies* wore goatskins as costumes. Have you seen a *tragedy* about an actor who wears a goatskin? Now that would be tragic.

tragedy

"Life's **tragedy** is that we get old too soon and wise too late."
—Ben Franklin (U.S. statesman)

Trekkie One devoted to the futuristic 1970s television series, *Star Trek*, is known as a *Trekkie*. Although the true fan of this science-fiction program would rather be called a *Trekker*, a *Trekkie* enjoyed watching the treks (or journeys) of Captain James T. Kirk, Commander Spock, Scotty, and the other members of the starship *Enterprise*. How many members of your family are *Trekkies*?

Trekkies wave hello at a Star Trek convention.

trivia The ancient Romans would often meet and converse at the spot where three (*tri*) ways or roads (*via*) met. Because their conversations were usually no more than small talk or gossip, the place where they met, *trivia*, became associated with unimportant matters. Today *trivia* also refers to little-known, insignificant facts. The popularity of the board game *Trivial Pursuit* attests to the importance of the unimportant matters of *trivia*.

truck *Truck* was formed by combining the ancient words *trochos* (wheel) and *trechein* (to run). Two hundred years ago, a *truck* was a cart that

Truck

carried items to be *trucked* (exchanged or traded). Less than a century ago, the word *truck* was extended to mean the motor vehicle we know today. Will *trucks* be around in another century? That is not a trick *truck* question!

T-shirt With small sleeves and a round collar, the *T-shirt* (or tee shirt), originally an underwear garment, was so named because when spread out flat, it resembles the letter T. The *T-shirt* is made in more colors than its initial white and is used for more than just a piece of underwear. This piece of clothing is also used as a place to store one's cigarettes or glasses and as a message board for both its wearer and advertisers. It is not unusual to see the names and logos of high schools, colleges, sports teams, or music groups on *T-shirts*. Sweat shirts and muscle shirts have also been part of the American fashion scene. The *T-shirt* was, and still is, the most popular item of clothing. After all, for many wearers, these *T-shirts* fit them to a tee.

T-shirts

Tuesday The "day of Tiw," or *Tuesday*, was named after Tiw, the mythological Germanic god of war. The French remember Tiw's Roman equivalent, Mars, with their word for *Tuesday*, Mardi. Fat *Tuesday*, or *Mardi Gras*, is the last day before Lent, the forty days of fasting and prayer. It is also the last day of the *carnival*, Latin for "Flesh, farewell!" Let's not fight over *Tuesday*'s history!

turf (*slang*) During the 1930s, *turf* was jive talk for sidewalk or street. By the 1950s, *turf* entered the slang vocabulary of youth gangs where it designated the territory controlled by a gang. *Turf* wars often included a rumble (violent fighting between gangs) as gangs fought to protect their *turf*. In the second half of the 1900s, Astro*turf* (named for the Houston Astrodome stadium), the durable synthetic carpet used in place of natural grass, was used in some baseball stadiums. Do astronauts have space wars over their astro*turf*?

turkey As long as 500 years ago, the British people spoke of the *turkey*, a bird that came from Guinea in Africa. Imported by English buyers from Turkish merchants, this guinea fowl was appropriately (or inappropriately) named *turkey*.

Wild turkeys, like the one above, were almost wiped out in the early 1900s. Today there are wild turkeys in every state except Alaska.

turquoise

Because these beautiful, semiprecious greenish-blue gems supposedly came to western Europe through Turkey, *turquoise*, the French form of the word, seems an appropriate name. Now we have talked turkey about the history of *turquoise*.

Like the name for the guinea fowl, or turkey, the name *turquoise* is derived from the word Turkey.

umpteenth *(slang)* "I am telling you for the *umpteenth* time!" How many is *umpteen*? There is no specific number associated with *umpteenth*. It simply means a "very large" number! In early *Morse Code*, M or *umpty*, meant "large" or "many." In turn, perhaps the letter M, the Roman numeral for 1,000, adds to the idea of a large number. With the addition of *teen*, meaning ten, the number *umpteenth* could be many thousands. Maybe even *umpteenth* thousands!

Uncle Sam The name *Uncle Sam* originated during the War of 1812 as a humorous expansion of the initials U.S., the first letters of the two words making up United States. So many governmental military vehicles were marked "U.S." that people expanded the U.S. to *Uncle Sam*. The cartoons of Thomas Nast, the

The Uncle Sam poster is best known as a recruitment ad.

well-known political cartoonist, popularized the figure of *Uncle Sam* sporting his high hat with its stars and stripes. Does your Uncle Sam look like the U.S. government's *Uncle Sam*?

underdog Most people would rather be the *top dog*, the most important or favorite, than the *underdog*, the one who is expected to lose. Memorable stories in sports and other areas featuring an underdog's victory are legendary. The biblical David, the underdog who used his slingshot, took care of the powerful Goliath. Some believe that this word for "one

I WANT YOU FOR U.S. ARMY

NEAREST RECRUITING STATION

at a decided disadvantage" is taken from an 1800s song entitled "The Under-Dog in the Fight." The song's lines include the words, "For my heart will beat, while it beats at all, For the underdog in the fight." Though some American pioneers sometimes enjoyed a good dogfight, they did have a heart for the dog on the bottom, the *under-dog*. At times the *underdog* was fortunately rescued from the jaws of death by a caring spectator. Perhaps that is why even today many people root for the *underdog*.

underdog

"The average American is for the **underdog**, but only on the condition that he has a chance to win."

—*Bill Vaughan (U.S. journalist and author)*

underhanded Through the years, dishonest players have sneakily held extra cards under the table during card games. Such illegal, *underhanded* tactics gave us today's adjective meaning secret or sly. The term *under the table* also means to perform an action in a secretive way. On the other hand, upper hand means to have an advantage. How often do *underhanded* tactics give card players the upper hand?

valedictorian In Latin,
valedictorian means "farewell." Students
at Harvard College, America's first
college (founded in 1636), chose a

valedictorian in 1759. Two decades later,
a student at the College of New Jersey
in Princeton delivered a *valedictorian*
speech. At today's high school and
college commencements (graduations),
the *valedictorian*, the highest achieving
senior, delivers the *valedictorian*
(farewell) speech after the salutatorian,
the second highest achieving
senior, delivers the salutatorian
(greeting) speech. Now say
"Farewell" to *valedictorian*.

Valedictorian giving farewell speach

Valley Girl

The speech of the teenage girls from the San Fernando Valley in suburban Los Angeles, California, gave rise to this popular and distinctive language during the early 1980s. Often the subject of ridicule, the *Valley Girl* combined many of the expressions used by surfers and added her own attitude to the words and expressions. Good things were *awesome*, *totally*, *super* or *to the max*, while bad things were *beastie* and *grisly*. These ills could be so *grody to the max* that they could make the Valley Girl exclaim, "*Gag me with a spoon!*" So, *fer sure*, learn this *gnarly* word and don't *barf me out*.

vandalize

The name *Vandal* means "the wanderer." Almost 2,000 years ago, the *Vandals* "wandered" through France, Spain, and Africa—killing people and destroying cities along the way. Years later, 80,000 *Vandals* captured Rome, Italy. Here they persecuted the Roman officials and citizens, plundered the buildings, and took the historical and cultural valuables with them. Today, to *vandalize* means "to purposely destroy or damage another's property." Thank the original wandering destroyers, the *Vandals*, for *vandalize*.

varsity

Today the *varsity* is the main team that represents a school in competitions such as athletic events, academic honors, and debates, to name a few. *Varsity* is a shortened form of "university." Even though *versity* was the original shortened form, *varsity* has been in the language for over a century and a half. Players on the jayvee or JV (junior *varsity*) teams usually move up to the *varsity*. In most universities, there is no scarcity of *varsity* competitors.

Vaseline®

In 1858, Robert A. Chesebrough, a Brooklyn chemist, observed that the oil workers near Titusville, Pennsylvania, had many cuts, bruises, and burns from their strenuous work pumping oil from the ground. In addition, he saw that these men would rub their hurt spots with a waxy substance from the pump rods that brought up the oil. Seeing the possible medical uses for this waxy substance, Chesebrough made a jell-like product from it. He patented this ointment made from petroleum and named it *Vaseline*®, combining the

Vaseline is a petroleum jelly, shown here.

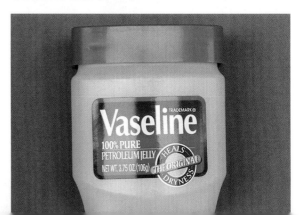

German word for water and the Greek word for olive oil. Fortunately, you do not have to drill the earth for your *Vaseline*. Just visit your local drugstore.

veejay

A video jockey (VJ or *veejay*) is an offshoot of *disc jockey*, or DJ, a term that has been around since the 1940s. This term for one who presents a program of pop videos, especially on television, has been part of the English language since the early 1980s. *Veejays* have appeared on MTV (Musical Television Video) since the television network's inception.

venom

Our modern-day word for poison, *venom*, can be traced back to Venus, the Roman goddess of love and beauty. According to mythology, *venenum* (*venom's* Latin ancestor) was the love potion Venus used to attract people to each other. But times do change! About 800 years ago, *venenum* was used to describe poison. What would lovely Venus say about this turn of events? She would probably have some *venomous* remarks.

The Portuguese man-of-war, above and below the water's surface, has a poison similar to a cobra's venom.

vermicelli The next time you eat *vermicelli*, the very thin pasta, remember that this Italian word means "little worms," from the Latin word for "worm, maggot, or crawling insect." Hungry, anyone?

Bowl of vermicelli—the spaghetti, not the worm!

vibes (*slang*) The All-American-looking Beach Boys, a 1960s (and beyond) California musical group, recorded a very popular song called "Good Vibrations." Here vibrations meant sensations or feelings. The

hippies of that era shortened the word vibrations to *vibes*, and so another word was added to the slang vocabulary! *Vibes* designated those instinctive sensations that allowed people to know what is going on around them. Although the Beach Boys had good vibrations, many others, unfortunately, suffered from bad *vibes*. Such is life!

villain

In the early 1300s, a *villein* was a member of one of the lower classes. Technically speaking, this *villein* was a "low-born rustic." Though he may have been considered a free man, he was a serf bound to his *lord's villa* or estate. Unfortunately, the upper crust of society (aristocrats) looked down on this *villein*, and by the late 1300s, he had developed a reputation of one having low morals and bad manners. Today, a *villain* is "an unprincipled scoundrel, often looked down upon as the cause of some problem." By the 1800s, a *villain* was also the name given to the "bad guy" in theatrical productions. Can you name some of literature's most famous *villains*?

> ## villain
>
> "The more successful the **villain**, the more successful the picture."
>
> —Alfred Hitchcock (English movie director)

vodka

The Russians gave us the word for *vodka*, the colorless alcoholic drink that looks much like water. *Voda* is Russian for water. Through the ages, alcoholic beverages have been called the "water of life." So, *voda*, the Russian form of life's essential liquid, water, is the English *vodka*. Drinking too much *vodka* can make a person *intoxicated*. That is why people should not be rushing to drink this Russian concoction.

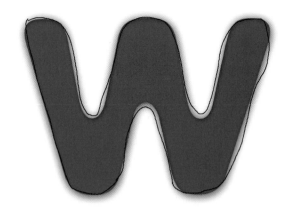

directly linked to President Nixon, were caught stealing Democratic National Committee information from a room in The *Watergate*. This action, including the attempted cover-up of these and other scandalous actions, led to Nixon's 1974 resignation.

The Watergate was the scene of one of the biggest political scandals in history. Other scandals since then have been compared to the Watergate scandal.

wannabe (*slang*) In the early 1980s, the word *wannabe*, slang for "want to be," was a disparaging name for one who wanted to be like a certain celebrity or type, especially regarding another's lifestyle or appearance. A *wannabe*, or *wanna-be*, often sought increased status or esteem by wanting to have the wealth, style, or prestige of other people. The slang *poser* was a synonym for *wannabe*. Would you ever want to be a *wannabe*? Let's hope not.

Watergate Located on the former docks of the Potomac River in Washington, D.C., The *Watergate*, a residential and office building, was the headquarters of the Democratic National Committee in 1972. The Democrats were working to elect George McGovern who was running against President Richard M. Nixon, a Republican, in the 1972 presidential campaign. On June 17, 1972, burglars,

Wednesday The ancients believed that the day of Woden, the modern name for *Wednesday*, was the best day to plant crops. Woden was the Norse (Norwegian) god of agriculture known for his foot speed and his eloquent speech. His Roman counterpart, Mercury, was the messenger of the gods. The French honored Mercury with Mercredi, French for *Wednesday*. Do farmers run to plant their crops on *Wednesdays*?

weird Six hundred years ago, *weird* meant "having the power to control fate." The word had earlier been used as a noun meaning "fate or destiny." The fate of William Shakespeare's title character Macbeth is influenced by the three witches known as the three Fates. The use of *weird* as an adjective for fate appears in English literature in the early 1600s. About 200 years after that, *weird* became a synonym for "odd, magical, or fantastic." Depending on which definition of *weird* is used, both the strange-acting person and the magician do *weird* things.

whipping boy Since the members of royalty were considered sacred, English princes were not allowed to be flogged or whipped. So until about 400 years ago, English princes often had *whipping boys*, usually commoners about the prince's age, who took the punishments or whippings that the prince deserved for his misbehaviors. A word similar in meaning to *whipping boy* is *scapegoat*, one punished for others' misdeeds.

white elephant A *white elephant* is a sometimes useless possession that is often costly to its owner. Any object (a large house, for example) that is too costly to maintain and cannot be sold because of its apparent uselessness (and expense) is referred to as a *white elephant*. Today, in America, a white elephant is also the name given to an object that the owner no longer wants, though it can still be useful and valuable for someone else. Long ago, the King of Siam owned *white elephants* that were considered sacred to him. These rare beasts were not work animals as many other elephants were. They were quite expensive to maintain since they ate well and needed the finest of care. Because these white elephants did no work, they were more of a burden than anything else. Legend has it that the Siamese king, wanting to punish a person, would give him a *white elephant*. This useless animal, needing costly care, would financially ruin the person. So unlike the *white elephant* itself, this story is neither useless nor expensive.

windfall

A *windfall* is any unexpected gain or stroke of good fortune. If you inherit several million dollars, you have had a *windfall*. The same is true of a charity organization that receives an unexpected gift of several million dollars from a benefactor. Where did the word *windfall* originate? Hundreds of years ago in England, a rule stated that commoners could not cut down trees, but they could keep any trees or branches that fell when the wind blew them down. This *windfall*, or unexpected fortune, of wood surely benefited the common folk. Would you rather have a million dollars or a few branches for your *windfall*?

wired

(*slang*) Since the 1980s, *wired* or *wired up* means to be in a state of nervous excitement or to be tense or edgy. People who drink too much coffee are often described as being over-stimulated or *wired*. In the vocabulary of narcotics, *wired* means to be intoxicated by drugs. Essentially, either of these *wired* conditions is similar to the electrical charge sent through a wire. Another meaning of *wired* describes the condition of wearing a device or *wire* to *eavesdrop* on another. More recently, *wired* designates the condition of being "hooked up to the Internet." Hopefully, all of this information on *wired* will not cause you to be *wired up*.

witch's brew

Through the ages, witches were thought to have supernatural powers. Often, these women seemed to be brewing some mysterious concoction—whether it be a remedy for some minor illness or something more powerful for another perhaps more important (maybe evil) dilemma. What was in these mixtures was quite another story. Even kings, such as William Shakespeare's Macbeth, were influenced by witches. The three witches in *Macbeth* threw the animals' poisoned inner organs, including a frog's toe, a dog's tongue, a lizard's leg, and more, in their cauldron (large iron pot). Today, a *witch's brew* means any strong mixture prepared with mysterious purposes.

workaholic

The suffixes "-*holic*" and "-*aholic*" had their beginnings in the 1960s and 1970s when many people began to be consumed with various activities. Those people obsessed or addicted with either serious or humorous addictions were given appropriate names. So one probably kids the choco*holic*, the soccer*aholic*, the ice cream*aholic*, or the shop*aholic*. More serious treatment is given to the alco*holic*, one addicted to alcohol, and the work*aholic*, one addicted to work. Fortunately, support groups have been formed to help these individuals.

During income tax filing time, many accountants become workaholics to get the forms in by the due date.

workfare

In the late 1960s, the U.S. government instituted a policy called *workfare* requiring welfare recipients (those given money by the government) to perform some work in exchange for government assistance. Those who *coined* the name *workfare* probably did so with the word welfare in mind. Do you think that *workfare* is fair? Work on that question for a while.

X-ray During one of his experiments in 1895, German physicist Wilhelm Konrad von Roentgen found that radiation could pass through objects that were supposedly impenetrable to ordinary light. Puzzled by this finding, Roentgen called his discovery X-*strahlen*, German for *X-rays*. Why? For Roentgen, the nature of this short wave ray was a mystery. Knowing that *X* is used as the symbol for the unknown in math, what better choice could he make? Today, *X-rays* are also called roentgen rays.

X-rays are very helpful to doctors in finding out what's wrong.

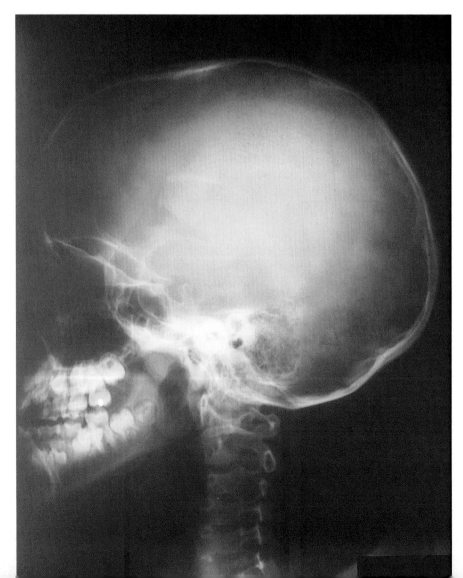

cruises and races. The original *yachts* were pirate ships (*yaughts*) that were named after a speedy German pirate ship called the *jacht*. In the 1700s, the British changed the spelling of yaughts to *yachts* and used the boats for pleasure cruising. What a steal to have the pleasure of knowing the history of the word *yacht*.

yacht Many people who love boating would love to own a *yacht*, a boat used primarily for pleasure

Many wealthy people who enjoy boating own a yacht.

yacht

"Anyone who has to ask about the annual upkeep of a **yacht** can't afford one."

—J.P. Morgan (U.S. financier)

yen A *yen* is a strong desire for something. You could have a *yen* for lasagna, for a house in the mountains, or for a better bicycle. Though neither "urgent" nor "immediate" is included in *yen*'s definition today, that was not the case when *yen* became a word. During much of the 1700s and 1800s, people in China, some native Chinese and visitors alike, smoked the powerful drug called opium. They so loved the effects of this addictive substance that they developed a *yinyan* or urgent craving for more. These smokers needed an immediate fix. Traders from foreign nations made large profits by selling opium. By the mid-1800s, Chinese immigrants had brought the expression "*in-yan*" (craving for opium) with them to the United States. Gradually shortened to *yan* and then to the present-day *yen*, the word still means a powerful craving!

yoga Sanskrit, the ancient language of India, included the word *yoga* for "a yoking with the divine." Originally, *yoga* was a system of Hindu philosophy whose purpose was personal physical and mental freedom and the union with the Supreme Being. *Yoga* included intense concentration, deep meditation, controlled breathing, and various body positions. *Yoga* as a form of meditation and physical exercise is still practiced by many people today.

Yoga class

yuppie Since there were many *Y*oung *U*rban (city) *P*rofessionals in the money-conscious 1980s, the word *yuppie* (the suffix "-pie" was added to the first letters of the three words) was invented. *Yuppies* were usually ambitious, financially successful people in their 20s and 30s who lived in or near a major city. Some could even be called *workaholics*. The suffix "-pie" also gave rise to *preppies*, those associated with the success, wealth, and dress of prep schools, and *hippies*, those who turned away from the mainstream of society (and sometimes turned toward communes, drugs, and the psychedelic) in the 1960s. Perhaps the *yuppies* could coin more "-pie" ending words—for a fee, of course.

These yuppies are dressed for success.

zany

In the 1500s, Italian theater developed a popular form of comedy known as comedia dell'arte. One of the less important characters was the fool or clown servant who would imitate the actions of his master. This very silly character was named Zanni, taken from Gianni, the shortened form of Giovanni (John). Today *zany* means any silly person or the nonsensical actions of that person. Many enjoy the *zany* antics of the Three Stooges, that pie-throwing, face-slapping trio.

zap

(*slang*) It seems that *zap*, possibly a combination of *z*(ip) and (sl)*ap*, was initially used in the comic strips of the 1940s. When a comic strip character struck, stunned, defeated, or killed another, he *zapped* that person (or thing). *Zap*, to kill, was unfortunately a popular word during the Vietnam War. Then, with the emergence of the microwave in the 1970s, *zap*, meaning "to microwave," was added to our vocabulary. Lastly, the 1980s gave us *zap*, meaning "to erase electronically," as in "The absent-minded worker *zapped* the computer's files."

zest

Exactly where the French found their word for *zest* (great enjoyment), no one knows for sure. Their *zeste* originally meant an "orange or lemon peel." These peels were added as flavoring for food and drinks. By the 1700s, *zeste* became "a quality that adds enjoyment to anything," not just food and drinks. Presently, *zest* refers to keen enjoyment of any activity. *Zesty* is the adjective form of *zest*. How *zesty* are orange peels? Mmm...

> ## zest
>
> "**Zest** is the secret of all beauty. There is no beauty that is attractive without **zest**."
>
> —Christian Dior (French designer)

zigzag

Have you ever *zigzagged* when trying to avoid being caught in a game of Tag. Thank the Germans for *zigzag* ("to make frequent sharp turns from side to side"). *Ziche* (to dodge about) and *zacke* (a jagged edge) are the two probable words that make up our English word *zigzag*. The first time *zigzag* was used in English was in reference to the planning of the garden path (a *zigzag* pattern). Here is a tongue-twister for you to try. Ziggy has *zigzagged* his way through the garden's zinnias.

Zip code

In the early 1960s, the U.S. Post Office introduced the Zip code, a series of digits representing a particular area used in addressing mail. This five-digit code helped to deliver mail more effectively. *Zip* is an acronym for *Zoning Improvement Plan*. More recently, four digits have been added to make the Zip code nine digits. Now postal workers can zip through the mail even faster.

Before mailing out a letter, please be sure that you have written the right address and *Zip code*.

To Find Out More

"A Word with You" **http://www.wordwithyou.com**

"Behind the Name —The Etymology and History of First Names"
http://www.behindthename.com

"Etymologically Speaking" **http://www.westegg.com/etymology**

"Knowledge Master Weekly Quiz"
http://www.greatauk.com/wqetymology.html

"ML Literature and Language Arts: Idiom of the Week"
http://www.mcdougallittell.com/disciplines/lang.cmf

"Origin of Phrases" **http://members.aol.com./MorelandC/PhrasesIndex.htm**

"Speaking of Language" **http://www.factmonster.com/ipka/A0769282.html**

"Take Our Word for It" **http://www.takeourword.com**

"The Word Detective" **http://www.word-detective.com**

"What Is Etymology?" **http://www.fun-with-words.com/etymology.html**

"Wilton's Word & Phrase Origin" **http://www.wordorigins.org**

"Word for Word" **http://plateaupress.com.au/wfw/wfwindex.htm**

"World Wide Words" **http://worldwidewords.org/weirdwords/index.htm**

"Ye Olde English Sayings" **www.rootsweb.com/~genepool/sayings.htm**

"Your Dictionary.com" **http://www.yourdictionary.com**

Almond, John. *Dictionary of Word Origins: A History of the Words, Expressions, and Clichés We Use.* Secaucus, NJ: Carol Publishing Group, 1995.

Ayto, John. *The Dictionary of Word Origins.* New York: Arcade Publishing, 1993.

Barnett, David, and Allan A. Metcalf. *America in So Many Words: Words That Have Shaped America.* Boston: Houghton-Mifflin, 1999.

Funk, Charles. *2107 Curious Word Origins, Sayings and Expressions from White Elephants to Song Dance.* LaVergne, TN: Ingram Book Company, 1993.

Hendrickson, Robert. *The Facts on File Encyclopedia of Word and Phrase Origins* (Facts on File Writer's Library). New York: Checkmark Books, 2000.

McCrum, Robert, William Cran, (contributor), and Robert MacNeill, (contributor). *The Story of English.* New York: Penguin USA Books, 1993.

The Merriam—Webster New Book of Word Histories. Springfield, MA: Merriam-Webster, 1991.

Popkin, David. *Vocabulary Energizers: Stories of Word Origins.* Nashville, TN: Hada Publications, 1988.

Room, Adrian. *The Fascinating Origins of Everyday Words.* Lincolnwood, IL: NTC Publishing Group, 1997.

Simpson, J.A., and Edmund Weiner, eds. *The Oxford English Dictionary* (Second Edition, 20 Volume Set). New York: Oxford University Press, 1989.

(**Boldface** page number indicates illustrations.)